The Transformal Organization

A Business Paradigm for the 1990s

The Transformal Organization

A Business Paradigm for the 1990s

Louis DeThomasis, FSC
President, Saint Mary's College of Minnesota

William Ammentorp
Professor, Policy Studies, University of Minnesota

Mary C. Fox
Dean, School of Business, Saint Mary's College of Minnesota

With a Foreword by James E. Cayne, President, Bear Stearns, Inc.

Published by   The Metanoia Group
                Saint Mary's College of Minnesota
                700 Terrace Heights
                Winona, Minnesota 55987-1399

Table of Contents

Foreword

Like most executives, I spend a good deal of time looking to the management literature for ideas and practices which might help my organization deal with emerging problems. I must say that I've been almost uniformly disappointed. The textbooks and papers coming out of business schools are too far removed from the real world of global business. They also contain rigid frames of reference that fail to fit the issues I face each day. On the other hand, the popular books and magazines are so superficial that they are almost dangerous to modern managers.

What is particularly frustrating is that there seems to be no truly new ideas as to how the business enterprise might be organized and managed. What I see are old principles, cloaked in the newest buzzwords of Wall Street, and tiresome cycles of change from current forms of organization to ones that were rejected only a few years ago. Digging in these management landfills is, in my judgment, a good way to contract a disease that will prove to be fatal in the rarified business climate of the 1990s.

Given these experiences with business writing, I confess that I had little interest in reviewing *The Transformal Organization*. Imagine my surprise when I found that it discussed the global business enterprise from a perspective which made sense out of the problems on my desk. The authors struck a responsive chord in me when they made the case for a new business paradigm—this is exactly what the contemporary executive is wanting. We must have new ways of thinking about business activities if we are to shoulder the responsibility of shaping a new world order. As the authors point out, it's far too early to crow about the victory of capitalism; instead we had better look to the *transforming* of our institutions and practices so that they can respond to the social and political turmoil that bubbles around us every day.

The Transformal Organization goes well beyond this appealing notion. It makes sense of a variety of important developments in business practice and shows how they can be integrated into a paradigm which is likely to work in the nineties. By making the case for value and quality, the book gives business leaders a focus on what their organizations are about. When these objectives are placed in the information-rich context of today's business, we can readily see how a new generation of executives must act and how they should be trained. In fact, *The Transformal Organization* is an ideal catalyst for changing the ways we train managers. If it were to be the required introductory text in our business schools, we could expect to see graduates with the knowledge and insight to make our corporations exciting and vital.

This is also an inspirational book. The authors recognize that business organizations are as much about myths and metaphors as they are about money. They take the position, which I applaud, that it is imagination which provides the driving force for the transformal organization. It is imagination which energizes executives and enables them to motivate those who work with them. It is imagination which points to evolving paradigms which can ensure the future of the corporation. And, it is those with imagination who visualize the organization as an integral part of a global society where democratic capitalism and social justice can flourish.

To the aspiring young manager I would say, build yourself a new business paradigm so that you can *transform* the company where you will be working. Look to this book for the framework on which that paradigm can be constructed. Keep the issues it raises at the front of your thinking so that your decisions are always in step with the issues of the times and consistent with the fundamental goal of business—to improve the quality of life for all people.

To practicing managers I would say, study this book and look for ways that your organization can operate under the transformal paradigm. This is, I believe, good advice and a necessary condition for successful exercise of leadership in the years ahead. But, more than that, it is a call to executive imagination to find ways to release the tremendous energy of the capitalist system for the benefit of all those who hold a stake in our corporations.

James E. Cayne
President
Bear Stearns
New York

CHAPTER 1

The Business Environment of the 1990s

Strategy, Tactics and Paradigms

The paradigm shift we are advocating in this book could be dismissed as just another sales pitch. After all, isn't the notion of paradigm change one of the hottest fads in the management consultant marketplace? And, aren't there countless speeches and articles which promise more profits with new paradigms?

If all we were about was to join in the feeding frenzy of trendy management thought, readers should consider other uses of their time. However, our study of the business environment of the 1990s leads to the inescapable conclusion that business as usual will put most companies at risk of failure in the future. There are some solid reasons for considering new organization designs and revolutionary approaches to management. These reasons are so compelling that they make the case for shifts in current business paradigms which assist business men and women in developing effective strategies for the nineties.

Most businesses are entering the decade of the nineties with a tactical rather than a strategic orientation. Their managers are moving into a global marketplace by making incremental changes in business practices. They hope that their organization can learn from its experiences and that individual and corporate behavior can be shaped to conditions in the global economy. This is a sound business tactic, and many organizations will experience short-run successes by "tweaking" their current structures and activities.

"Tweaking" is, however, a flawed strategy in that it fails to recognize the nature of the global business environment. Global business is not merely an extension of national economic activity. It is not carried out under the jurisdiction of any particular set of government rules. In fact, the rules constantly change as new problems and conflicts emerge. Global business does not conform to any particular national model of corporate structure. Instead, it continually devises new forms of organization to meet the demands of particular markets.

Global business in the 1990s is conducted in what Emery and Trist called a turbulent field (1965). This is an environment where dynamic forces outside the organization are making major changes in social, economic and political systems. These changes are of such magnitude and direction that they cannot be predicted by managers. Hence, familiar business practices are unlikely to meet with much success and organizations lose control over their exchanges with economic, social and political actors in their environments.

To cope with the turbulent environments of the nineties, business leaders will need to devise new types of organizations. These will be based on values and premises quite different from those in force today. These organizations will express a business paradigm which takes explicit account of the turbulent global environment. This new paradigm will draw on the best features of communist, socialist and capitalist systems to develop a view of economic activity which is able to address the major global issues of the next decade.

The paradigm will necessarily focus on the whole range of resources available to the organization so that each is used in productive ways. As Peter Drucker noted ten years ago, "Managers thus have to manage separately the productivity of all four key resources: capital, crucial physical resources, time, and knowledge. . . . it is the steady increase in the productivities of all resources in their specific institution to which managers must commit themselves in turbulent times" (1980, p. 28). By taking account of the productivity of each resource, managers can vary their "mix" to better fit the organization to its business environment.

FIGURE 1.1

TURBULENCE: THE PARADIGM REALITY CLASH

The turbulence facing managers in the nineties is the result of a clash between three sets of forces. Existing Business Paradigms come up against National and Global Realities to create a set of circumstances in which old rules fail to hold and new threats and opportunities are created daily. These forces are diagrammed in Figure 1.1 where we show them impinging on the central *"turbulent cloud"* of the Business Environment.

Inside each arrow, are the causal factors which, we believe, will be the major sources of environmental turbulence in the nineties. To be sure, there are others which could be mentioned, but what we show in Figure 1.1 is sufficient to make the case for a new business paradigm. We can see how this case unfolds by considering the probable effects of our causal factors on the business environment of the next decade.

Little Boats and Clear Sailing

The Existing Paradigms in the minds of business leaders result in an optimistic view of the nineties. Most leaders believe it will be a time of growth and opportunity where expanding world markets will ensure profitability for all well-managed firms (See esp. "Today's Leaders Talk About Tomorrow," *Fortune*, March 26, 1990). There is a rosy glow about these perspectives which see America as the primary actor in the new global economic and political systems.

Not surprisingly, the Existing Paradigms are built on recent business experience. There is something about a decade of sustained growth and the survival of a stock market crash that solidifies experience and makes it a stable launching point for the ventures of the nineties. The fact of these achievements makes us vulnerable to the error of assuming that what worked in the past will be successful in the future. We can see this assumption at work in each of the factors included in our Existing Paradigms as well as some significant "minuses" which call it into question.

Structure: The mega-businesses created by the leveraged buyouts of the eighties represent diversified strength which is impervious to environmental turbulence. The economics of size help each constituent venture in the mega-business smooth variations in its own marketplace and give it the financial basis for capturing ever-increasing market share.

The mega-business can also enlist the management talent needed to be competitive in a global economy. It is able to test a wide range of management practices which enhance its capacity to adapt to new environmental conditions. In addition, the mega-business has the knowledge and experience which make it the most favored competitor.

On the Minus Side: The very size of these mega-businesses may be testing the limits of corporate control. By assuming that "management is managing" these businesses have distanced management from production and marketing so that they have legions of financial analysts and few managers who understand what the organization is about.

The mega-business is weak in a more fundamental way. It captures the thinking of its managers and employees so that they come to believe that nothing outside the organization counts for very much. Thus, these businesses are insensitive to political, social and cultural issues and are often surprised by the power such issues have over people.

Even though the mega-business has sophisticated communication and control systems, it is slow to react to change. In the dynamic environment of the nineties, many of these organizations will be foundering on waves of change which they have not perceived and are unable to ride.

Mega-business also violates the general principle that business organizations exist to serve the consumer. These organizations are servants of financial interests, and fiscal health takes precedence over consumer concerns. In effect, the mega-business is like a small nation governed by a benevolent dictatorship; a nation which is ill-prepared to compete in the high-stakes, high-speed global economy.

Finance: New York is the center of global finance and all the important deals are cut on Wall Street. As a result, no business venture of any significance can be set in motion without the involvement of American banks and investors. These were the facts of the seventies and eighties and there are no good reasons to suspect that they will change in the near future.

This conclusion is supported by the capacity of the United States to manage its national debt. Economists have noted that the 1986 federal budget deficit amounted to about 5% of GNP. In 1989, this was reduced to 2.5% and there is the belief that continued GNP growth will further shrink this proportion to less than 1%. In other words, sustained growth will enable the U.S. to play a dominant role in the world economy.

On the Minus Side: The world financial market is no longer conducted in the Wall Street store. It is already globalized by international flows of money and computer-assisted trading of commodities and securities. This means that the real financial power is no longer under national controls. Instead, it is vested in the market mechanisms of global financial systems which are impervious to the control of any participating nation.

Although summary statistics tend to support the notion that national finances are under control, there is some very disturbing evidence to the contrary. Deficit reduction targets are met, not by real cuts, but by manipulation of accounts and "off budget" expenditures. More to the point, the federal government appears to be unable to determine its exact obligations. In the case of the savings and loan bailout, official estimates of costs were at $40 billion in January of 1989. This number had grown to a "worst case" estimate of $120 billion by May of 1990 and something like $300 billion six months later.

The more damaging aspect of national debt is the extent to which it forces government into business. As a result of the S&L bailout, the federal government is now the world's largest property owner. This puts government in direct competition with private enterprise and makes it impossible to get an accurate picture of the financial strength of the nation.

Technology: There is a widely-held assumption that technology holds the solution for most of the world's problems. Again, the record is impressive. The health of much of the world's population can be traced to medical technology; agricultural productivity has been increased tremendously by the successes of the Green Revolution; standards of living in most Western nations have been increased beyond any expectation by the products and services made possible through modern technology.

This hopeful dependence on technology is presently centered on the computer revolution of the seventies and eighties. If this technology achieves anywhere near its expected potential, it can improve virtually every aspect of life—from the day-to-day activities of living to the most complex production and service operations. Since the United States was at the forefront of this development, it's reasonable to expect that information technology will propel the American ship of state in the years ahead.

On the Minus Side: The point must be made that the technological marvels of recent decades have been purchased by using up non-renewable resources. Hydrocarbon fuels have been burned as if the globe were a huge reservoir; agricultural lands have been managed as if they were able to regenerate themselves; scarce materials have been used briefly and consigned to the junk heaps of industrial civilization. It's abundantly clear that technology cannot continue on this course without drowning Western man in sophisticated garbage.

There's a second flaw in the technology-as-savior argument. That is, technology has been increasingly used to enhance the material standard of living of a relatively small fraction of the world's population. It has also been directed at producing the materials of war rather than the stuff of peace. This means that tremendous amounts of technological capital have been forever lost.

Management: America, as the nation that invented management, is in the best position to exploit its "installed base" of managers. These are individuals who have been trained by world-class business schools and find themselves at the controls of mega-business organizations. Their experience in directing decades of economic growth, when taken together with the organizational innovations they have introduced, is powerful intellectual capital which can be used to invest in the global economy.

These managers have not limited their skills to economic activities. They have directed the full range of organized human endeavor including non-profit corporations and government agencies. They have done this with a remarkable degree of professionalism and a true interest in the effects of their work on those they serve.

On the Minus Side: Despite the impressive record of American managers, there are some significant soft spots which have emerged in recent years. There is a substantial amount of corruption which goes against the professionalism mentioned above. There is a narrow focus on personal goals with little concern for the interests of employees and consumers. And, there are many managers who know little about the activities they supervise and care little about their long-term impact on the organization and the society.

These managers are not particularly adept at building and operating business organizations in the global economy. They are likely to be outperformed by their Japanese or German colleagues and outmaneuvered in negotiations with Eastern bloc diplomats. They are parochial in their points of view with little understanding of other cultures and less capacity to engage those who do not speak English.

Politics: The most limiting of our Existing Paradigms is that of democratic capitalism as practiced in the United States. Most business leaders believe that good old U.S. capitalism defeated communism in open economic combat and that American managers will replace commissars as benevolent bullies on the global playground. This leads to overconfidence in the political processes and systems of the U.S. and to the assumption that all nations will adopt these practices sooner or later.

On the Minus Side: As a part of this paradigm, business men and women in the U.S. have come to depend upon government to provide for competitive advantage. That is, by lobbying for special interests, business leaders have been able to enhance the profitability of their companies without competing in the open market. In addition, capitalist governments are direct actors in many markets as we noted in the case of S&L properties. These governments also buy significant amounts of goods and services directly from businesses so that they act like rather large consumers. Consequently, business leaders are continually selling in this market and are shaping their products and services to a buyer who is not concerned about the scarcity of money.

The symbiotic relationship between capitalists and political capitalism leads to an uncritical acceptance of the status quo. The capitalistic system of government cannot be questioned because too many have a stake in its persistence "as is." Its value base is rooted in these experiences and deals and is so deeply ingrained in all actors that nobody can conceive of adaptations that may be needed to make capitalism work in another culture.

These Existing Paradigms cloud the thinking of business and political leaders. They are what we characterize as the "little boat" view of the world. Each person at the rudders of these "boats" is steering according to charts which are, as we shall see, badly out of date. They had better heed Benjamin Franklin's admonition, "Little boats should stay near shore."

A Breeze of National Reality

Turbulence is always observable in reality. We see changes in our business environments in the form of new issues which rise and fall with turbulent frequency. This does not mean that our view of reality is unimportant. Quite the contrary; it is the dynamic flow of these realities which business leaders must track in order to understand turbulence and cope with it (Drucker, 1989). We can demonstrate the truth of this principle by considering some of the more significant National Realities of the nineties.

Demography: There is a growing consensus among business and political leaders that the most important National Reality of the nineties is demography. There are major changes already under way in the composition and location of the U.S. population. These will mature in the next decades to create a society which is quite different from the one we know today. It will be older, ethnically diverse, economically polarized and geographically divided. These will be conditions of such magnitude that no social institution or business will be able to function without taking them into account.

Anyone who has read the national press knows that America is aging and that the 65+ age group is the fastest growing segment of U.S. population. There is also the realization that this group will require services which are increasingly costly and likely to strain the fiscal capacity of both national and state governments. What few of these readers have grasped is the fact the whole age distribution is restructuring. Baby boomers are concluding their careers and using their considerable resources to extract the benefits of their working years. Their children are attending colleges with ever-greater frequency in the hope that they, too, will be able to maintain parental standards of living.

But the children of privilege are outnumbered by those less fortunate. Minorities who still have limited access to opportunity are growing much more rapidly than the white population and they will replace the Baby Boomers as the working majority in the future. These will be less well trained workers with limited economic resources and they will be asked to support the retirements of the very persons who have failed to deliver on the promise of opportunity.

What these developments will do is increase the divisions between those who have and those who have not. These divisions are already showing up in the distribution of wealth—10% of Americans hold more wealth than the other 90% (Levy, 1989). We also see these discrepancies in income; in 1987, the richest 5% of American families earned nearly 17% of all income while the poorest 20% of families earned less than 5% of national income. This is an economic condition that has had catastrophic impacts on markets in the past. It is also social dynamite that can explode our cities as it did in the late 1960s.

Work Force: The work force is where these demographic changes impact the business community most directly. The new workers of the nineties will be drawn from a population pool which is vastly different from that of the past. This pool will be drawn mainly from minority populations and will be increasingly ill-trained for jobs which will demand ever-higher levels of skill.

In a recent study of future work force conditions, the Hudson Institute estimated that 75% of all workers will need to be retrained by the year 2000. Further, the institute noted that 82% of today's jobs require four years of high school and that this proportion will increase to 87% by the year 2000 (Hudson Institute, 1989).

Against these objective demands, new entrants to the work force are ill-prepared. The National Assessment for Educational Progress (NEAP) states that less than 8% of 17-year-olds can deal effectively with scientific information and less than 7% can apply basic mathematical concepts. This is clearly a work force that does not provide a strong basis for the sort of productivity improvements needed in American businesses.

Debt: The other anchor holding the ship of economy back is that of corporate debt. Many of these obligations were taken on during the leverage buyout frenzy of the 1980s. While the bigger fish may have been dispersed by fiscal reality, they have left inordinately large debt burdens behind which corporations will carry far into the next millennium.

This not only places a draw on corporate cash flow, it diverts income from the investments needed to maintain ventures into the future. As business activities have become more complex and technologically dependent, they have come to make significant demands on investment. By virtue of corporate debt burdens, these investments are going begging for cash. As a recent National Science Foundation study shows, U.S. companies registered an average *increase* in spending for research and development of over 5% in 1987. In the same year, companies involved in leveraged buyouts averaged a 13% *decrease* in R&D spending. This is truly an eating of corporate seed corn which weakens the competitiveness of U.S. business—especially when it is compared with order-of-magnitude increases in R&D funding in Japan, France and West Germany.

Global Storm Warnings

These "breezes" may rock our corporate boats. They are, however, insignificant in comparison to the "gale-force winds" of global reality. These are winds that originate in the impact of humankind on the global environment; they are population-driven. This is clear in the five "realities" we have collected on the right-hand side of Figure 1.1.

Population: The world is now in a period when it is clear that the human population is growing exponentially. In 1968, world population was approximately 3.5 billion. In just over twenty years, that number has grown to 5.3 billion and will clearly result in 7 billion by the year 2000 (Ehrlich and Ehrlich, 1990). If we assume that this all started with Adam and Eve, we will reach a population level of 7 billion with 32 doublings. And, as demographers point out, "Filling all of the land surface of the planet Earth to the density of Manhattan would take us to only 10 more doublings from where we are (Keyfitz, 1977, p. 9).

Of greater importance than these physical limits to growth are the human consequences of population. The Ehrlich's research points out that in the last twenty years more than 200 million persons have died of hunger and disease and most of these were children. Since the explosive growth of populations is occurring in Third World countries where economic conditions are least robust, the misery related to growth is increasing even more rapidly. In 1988, 14 million children died of health-related causes. Most of these were Third World children who were the victims of the dual pressures of population growth and health-care programs restricted by governmental service of foreign debt (United Nations, 1988).

Unplanned population growth creates misery because humankind has a devastating impact on global ecology. Economic activity consumes resources, subsistence agriculture creates deserts out of rain forests and human activity taken as a whole generates heat from which there is no escape.

Pollution: This is the name for the impact of humans on their environment. When the *Club of Rome* warned of a potential catastrophic decline in population to occur in the early 2000s, it was basing its projections on the close link between pollution and population growth (Meadows, et.al., 1973). In the 1980s the gloomy predictions of *Limits to Growth* were rejected as it seemed that the impending crisis was being averted by such phenomena as energy conservation and recycling.

These now appear to have been responses which made only temporary corrections in the inevitable drift toward a world of decay and scarcity. The 1980s, which began so successfully, ended with the 11 million gallon oil spill in Prince William Sound, abandonment of an area the size of the state of Iowa as a result of the Chernobyl reactor accident, and a hole of unknown scope and consequence in the Earth's ozone shield. In its simplistic predictions, the Club of Rome was right; without a balance between humankind and the global ecology there is no future for the species.

Resources: This is the other side of the pollution coin. Population generates pollution because it uses resources to maintain and increase the material standard of living. The causal map of Figure 1.2 is taken from *Limits to Growth*; it shows the web of relationships in which humankind is caught.

In this drawing, arrows indicate the direction of causality; the variable at the tail of the arrow is the cause and the variable at the head is the effect. Plus signs (+) mean that causality operates in the same direction; increases in the cause variable lead to increases in the effect variable—

FIGURE 1.2

THE CAUSAL STRUCTURE OF GLOBAL REALITY

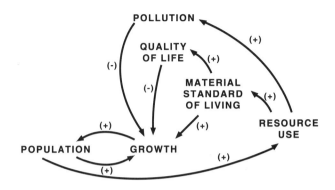

and decreases to decreases. Minus signs (-) mean that causality is reversed; increases lead to decreases and conversely.

The dynamic of Population is at the center of Figure 1.2. A positive Growth variable, (which is the case for human population,) leads to increases in Population—which lead to further increases in Growth. This is a relationship which feeds on itself to produce the population explosion.

Population is linked to Resource Use. Again, increases in Population lead to increases in Resource Use. This results in same-direction changes in the Material Standard of Living (MSL) of people. Then, increases in MSL are passed on to affect Growth. In this way, Resource Use can accelerate population growth.

The variable which controls explosive growth in this structure is Pollution. As Resource Use increases, due to Population growth, so does Pollution. This has a reverse effect on Growth since Pollution limits births and increases deaths. In this model, there is no escape from the inevitable control of human populations by the environments in which they live.

The consequence of this argument is to raise issues of global resource supply and to prioritize social and economic planning. Resources must be efficiently used to eliminate human misery and to limit pollution. And, they must be conserved so that those in finite supply are not depleted (*World Resources 1990–91*, 1990).

Quality of Life: There is one remaining variable in Figure 1.2 which we have not discussed. This is Quality of Life (QofL) which is a measure of the conditions under which people are living. It is shown as determined by Material Standard of Living and Pollution. These are variables which are both driven by Resource Use and their impact on QofL is opposite. MSL is directly (+) linked to QofL, and Pollution is inversely (-) linked to it. Thus, Quality of Life hangs in the balance depending upon how Resource Use is managed. If resources are squandered for short-run gains in standard of living, these gains may be wiped out over the longer run by pollution. On the other hand, careful stewardship over resources will trade off short-term gains in MSL in favor of a pollution-free environment.

This simple set of relationships uncovers some of the underlying paradoxes in human behavior. The Brazilian rain forest dweller slashes and burns the environment in order to improve MSL. As time passes, the pollution and environmental degradation resulting from these practices erase the short-term gains in QofL. The same motivation can be ascribed to the industrialist who squanders resources to build products which enhance the immediate MSL of customers. Again, the polluting consequences of inefficient production results in waste heaps and Love Canals which cause reductions in QofL of far greater magnitude than the short-run gains.

The forces diagrammed in Figure 1.2 are also at the base of political behavior. Those who control resources define MSL and QofL and, as a result, the allegiance of their constituents. When the decisions of political and economic actors result in serious imbalances in standard of living and quality of life, there is a potential for competition and aggression which can destroy the relationship between people and their environment.

Polarization: This occurs when large numbers of people begin to see that there are inequities in the distribution of quality of life. In controlled markets, this can lead to aggressive competition for resources and pressures for their efficient use. When these markets fail to keep pace with human expectations, they can polarize opinion between the "haves" and the "have nots."

This is the condition under which the vast majority of the world's population is living. The transistor radio and, now, television have made the majority aware of the standard of living of Western society. This awareness raises expectations which every government must address. However, the sheer numbers of people involved and the finite nature of resources mean that there is no way to meet the desires of most people.

The result is polarization which seeks meaning for inequity. This is often found in national conscience, ethnic heritage or religious conviction. These meanings further separate people from one another and make it impossible for collaborative problem solving. Thus, inequities increase and levels of hostility climb to the point where armed conflict is the only alternative.

When we consider that even those with the lowest MSL in the world are fully armed, the consequences of polarization are frightening. Western politicians have always assumed that arms were the means to control the less powerful. This, too, is paradoxical in that the less powerful now have weapons of mass destruction once reserved to a few nations. And, often those with a monopoly on force are unable to act, simply because they cannot use "final solution" weapons.

Business Solutions

After this gloomy review of reality, we'd like to offer some hope. Even though governments have shown themselves to be largely powerless to solve these problems, we believe that there is a future for humankind. It is, however, one which is defined in economics and tightly bound up with the way business is conducted in the immediate future. For, make no mistake, these are problems which must be solved in the nineties—or else there may be no working world order in the very near future.

There is a good deal of evidence that the solutions we are seeking go under the name of economic growth. Population is controlled only in those countries where quality of life has increased beyond some subsistence level. We show this in Figure 1.2 as a negative (-) relationship between QofL and Growth. Nations which have made it out of misery tend to show reductions in population growth which bring their dynamics into line with those of the developed world (George, 1977).

The increases needed in global quality of life can only be realized by sustained economic growth. But this is growth which must not be purchased at the expense of the ecology. This means that business leaders must manage the technology of production and supply so that it conserves resources and controls polluting effects.

In order to reach these goals, business women and men will need to view the world from a new perspective. This will be one which is sensitive to the interdependency of humankind and ecology and one which takes the longer view rather than a focus on short-term gains. This point of view is what we call the Transformal Paradigm because it *transforms* our view of business organizations and their impact on people and ecology. It also *transforms* our behavior and our organizations so that they are directed at improving the quality of life of all people.

In the next chapter, we offer a definition of paradigms which will help you understand how important they are. This is a definition which we will elaborate to the point where we can build our Transformal Paradigm and show you how it can be used to structure your own business activities.

References

Drucker, P. (1980) *Managing in Turbulent Times*. New York: Harper & Row.

Drucker, P. (1989) *The New Realities*. New York: Harper & Row.

Ehrlich, P. and Ehrlich, A. (1990) *The Population Explosion*. New York: Simon & Schuster.

Emery, F. and Trist, E. (1965) "The Causal Texture of Organizational Environments," *Human Relations*, 21-32.

George, S. (1977) *How the Other Half Dies*. Montclair, NJ: Allanheld Osmund.

Hudson Institute, *Workforce 2000*. New York: Hudson Institute.

Keyfitz, N. (1977) *Applied Mathematical Demography*. New York: J. Wiley.

Levy, F. *Dollars and Dreams: The Changing American Income Distribution*. (1989)

Meadows, D., et.al. (1973) *The Limits to Growth*. New York: Universe Books.

Oxford University, *World Resources 1990–91*. Oxford University Press.

United Nations (1988) *The World's Children*. Geneva, SW: United Nations.

CHAPTER 2

Myths, Models and Metaphors: The Dance of Business

In the late 1800s, the Paiute mystic, Wvoka, predicted a second coming of God who would appear only to the Indian people. God would make this choice because the white man had killed his Son and was no longer worthy of His attention. The new chosen people would be rewarded with the disappearance of the white man from Indian lands and buffalo would once again populate the grasslands of the Dakota.

The prophecy of Wvoka was at the heart of the Ghost Dance, a religious conversion which was rapidly accepted by many of the tribes of the Great Plains. Persecuted Indians found solace in the predictions of God's support for a return to happier times. Their confidence in the dance was enhanced by the assurance that warriors could wear a blessed garment which would turn the bullets of the white man's rifle.

History was to prove that the mythology of the Ghost Dance could not stand the test of reality. Even with God's help, the tribes could not vanquish the white man. And, the tragedy of Wounded Knee was to prove that no blessings could prevent genocide (Mooney, 1896).

Now, one hundred years later, the Plains of North Dakota seem to abound with evidence of the validity of the Ghost Dance. White populations are decreasing—at an increasing rate. Indian people are more numerous each year. And, there are proposals to turn western North Dakota into a grassland park where buffalo can freely increase in number (Popper and Popper, 1989).

These developments can be explained by Wvoka's religion. Each prediction of the Ghost Dance is coming true in an uncanny way. In fact, there are Indian businesses in North Dakota that are making bulletproof vests of Kevlar for the Pentagon!

If we take these observations at face value, we can see the appeal of mythology. Changes in population and economics are fully accounted for by the prophecies of the Ghost Dance. Even the detail of bulletproof garments has been foretold by the myth. If the uncritical observer accepts the Ghost Dance in full, he or she is able to tie all these events into a neat package. There are no unanswered questions.

However, mythical explanations work only where there are fortuitous coincidences between myth and reality. As these coincidences are more deeply analyzed, they tend to generate new questions which the myth cannot answer. For example, how does the Ghost Dance account for the interdependence of whites and Indians? How can its prophecies explain the fact that the Kevlar vests manufactured by Indians are to be worn almost exclusively by white warriors? Obviously, myth cannot be used to enhance understanding of the details of modern social life. It can only make us comfortable with superficial views of reality.

If we want to understand the social and economic forces at work in the Great Plains states, we need a more powerful explanatory system. We need to turn to an economic analysis of dry land agriculture; to the assessment of public defense policy; and to the value systems of white and Indian men and women. By bringing our knowledge to bear on these issues, we can not only explain the events of the past, we can make some reasonably accurate predictions of what is to come.

A Ghost Dance for Business

An understanding of mythology and explanation is especially important in the business community where managers and employees shape their work according to a standard set of ideas and principles which have stood the test of time. This specialized knowledge enables business men and women to design new products and services which will appeal to consumers; to resolve operational problems of production and distribution; and to identify new organizational forms in response to changes in the business environment. In fact, our knowledge about "what works" in business dictates the ways we approach problems and the ventures we'll attempt in the future.

This shared Dance of Business is what we mean by a paradigm. It's a way of looking at the business world to assess the threats and opportunities we face. It's also a collection of tested tools and techniques for solving problems. And, the paradigm is shared by most of the business community so that patterns of thought and action are remarkably similar across organizations and national boundaries.

The Dance of Business has its foundations in a set of beliefs about the world of commerce, the workings of economic systems, and the functioning of organizations. We find considerable evidence of these beliefs in the mythology of business. Thus, we have our Horatio Algers and our Lee Iacoccas who define the possible, and our "economic man" who makes only calculated decisions. The myths of their behavior capture the essential features of the ruling business paradigm in simple stories which picture the root causes of business activity.

One of the most powerful business myths is that applied to the Japanese culture where compulsive hard work resists the pull of consumption. This is the Japan That Can Say No (Morita, 1990) because it has mythical powers in its values, industry and an unlimited supply of cheap money. Like the Ghost Dance, this myth has experienced some problems in the nineties. Drastic declines in the Nikkei Average, increasing interest rates and devalued real estate invalidate the core mythology of Japanese economics. In addition, there is an awakening of the consumer which may strike at the cultural foundations of Japan Inc.

The Dance of Business also includes metaphors which describe the essential characteristics of business life. One of the best examples of business metaphor is that of finance as corporate lifeblood. This metaphor has led to concepts of financial health and illness and to fiscal diagnoses of corporate ills. By giving business men and women a well-known visual reference, metaphors help them get a grip on complex networks of cause and effect which would otherwise be impossible to comprehend.

Metaphors are even more powerful than myths for several reasons (Sterman, 1985). First, they are a pervasive part of our daily conversation. Every complex idea or system is reduced to metaphor to give us a common ground of understanding on which we can base the give and take of social and economic exchange. Second, metaphors help to select the key features of our environments. They point to the things we need to understand and control in order to function productively. By concealing the trivial, our metaphors make us efficient participants in a complex world. Finally, metaphors have the power to control what we do. They define reality for us and create behavior patterns that help us to deal with it.

The Dance of Business is, however, more than metaphor. There is a strength in its melody that links the generality of its metaphors to the reality of corporate life. The Dance helps us understand causality and to use it for the benefit of the corporation. This requires models which identify the key variables that must be managed in order to realize business objectives. These models take simple metaphors and enrich them with knowledge so that we can chart the course of our actions.

For example, we've translated the simple "lifeblood" metaphor into detailed spreadsheet models of business finance to help us determine what might happen as a consequence of decisions we might make. Such models are linked to the business activities of the corporation through a set of standardized accounting practices. As a result, the spreadsheet model is a true-to-life representation of the fiscal workings of the organization. So much so, that scenarios played out in the model are mirrored in corporate accounts and cash flows.

Myths, models and metaphors come together to define the ruling paradigm used by the majority of business leaders (Kuhn, 1970). This paradigm provides a foundation on which social, political and organizational behavior is based.

FIGURE 2.1

PARADIGMS AND BEHAVIOR

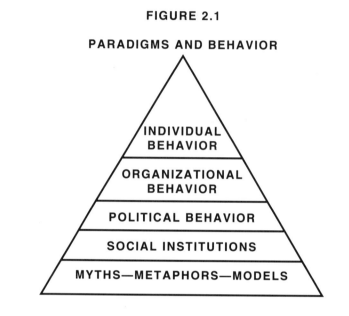

In Figure 2.1, we show that the ruling paradigm is articulated through political and social systems to direct the activities of business organizations. The organization, in turn, constrains the behavior of individuals by offering them roles and jobs. As these relationships mature, they are locked in place by laws, rules and social institutions so that there are effectively no other ways to "do business."

Why is a ruling paradigm such a powerful determinant of individual and collective behavior? The answer to this question lies in the capacity of the paradigm to define the rules of the game whereby individuals and groups gain access to the resources needed to improve well-being. Paradigms which prove to be effective in distributing the benefits of resource use to significant numbers of people become institutionalized in organizations and political systems. The practices supported by these systems have the force of law—assuring everyone a level playing field, or at least one with a known degree of unevenness. These rules go hand in hand with social institutions which set limits on individual action through interpersonal rewards and punishments. They are also supported by child rearing and educational practices which ensure a working relationship between the individual and the socioeconomic system.

In short, persons whose actions are in accord with the ruling paradigm will have access to jobs, positions and rewards. Those whose behavior deviates from the expectations set by the paradigm will be excluded and may even be punished if their activities are too extreme. As Figure 2.1 shows, social relationships growing out of the paradigm are the legitimate base for political structures. These, in turn, define the rules and controls which direct the social and economic activity of organizations. All of these forces bear on the individual so that only paradigm-appropriate behavior is likely to occur.

Different Drummers

Within nations and cultures, we can expect to find that most business is conducted out of a shared paradigm. Thus, everyone in the United States believes in the myths and metaphors of democratic capitalism and governs their behavior accordingly. The models of finance and operations associated with this paradigm ensure that one organization is very much like another on the other side of the country. In fact, within a culture like that of the United States, people can move from one organization to another without having to learn a whole new mythology or needing to come to grips with a new set of metaphors.

However, whenever we attempt to cross national and/or cultural boundaries it's clear that other business men and women aren't singing out of the same book. This is especially true when we try to cut deals with businesses organized under the communist paradigm. When Pepsi-Cola first attempted to enter the soft drink market in the USSR in the 1970s, they came face to face with a set of business practices which had no place for entrepreneurship and profitability. Even though Russians were quite interested in cola, they weren't willing to allow Pepsi's gains to be taken outside the country. The result was a vodka-cola deal which traded cola syrup for vodka to be sold in the United States.

In this example, the dancers (Pepsi and Smirnoff) had to turn to an older, mutually-recognizable business paradigm in order to do business.

Since each heard a different drummer, they needed to find an acceptable beat which could overcome the lock-step of competing paradigms. By accepting the general principles of barter, they were able to find the music and verse needed to organize a business venture which avoided the complications of fixed pricing and blocked currency characteristics of the communist paradigm.

The issues raised by different business drummers are not limited to deals like the vodka-cola connection. When we turn to the ecological problems described in Chapter 1, we are faced with the ultimate question, "Which paradigm is most likely to produce an efficient solution?" That is, which drummer—capitalist or communist—can do the best job of using the world's limited resources to the benefit of most people? The choice of drummer is probably the major challenge facing those who will make business, social and public policy in the 1990s. This is because the nation-state is becoming increasingly less viable as the sole policy maker of the future. As Peter Drucker notes, there are at least four potential policy-making entities in the transnational economy.

> The national state is one of these units, individual countries—especially the major, developed, non-communist ones—matter, of course. But increasingly decision-making power is shifting to a second unit, the region—the European Economic Community (EEC); North America; tomorrow perhaps a far eastern region grouped around Japan. Third, there is a genuine and almost autonomous world economy of money, credit, and investment flows. It is organized by information that no longer knows national boundaries. Finally, there is the transnational enterprise . . . which views the entire developed non-communist world as one market . . . both to produce and to sell goods and services (1989, p. 116).

Members of these groups will follow a "drummer of choice" as they interact in the transnational economy. If they all march off in different directions, the result will be a realization of the catastrophic predictions reviewed in Chapter 1. If, on the other hand, they come to a consensus on a viable business paradigm, they can approach the optimal use of world resources in addressing ecologically-sound goals. Thus, the "drummer question" is one of great importance; one which no business man or woman can neglect. As a first step toward an answer to this question, let's review the dances of three paradigms: capitalism, communism, and transformal. We'll do this by looking more closely at the central myths, metaphors and models of each. This will enable us to make a more accurate assessment of their candidacy for the Global Hit Parade of the 1990s.

The Paradigm of Democratic Capitalism

Mythology: The myth of capitalism is that hard work pays off. Diligent use of knowledge and skill enables every player to improve his or her standard of living and gives each the potential to accumulate capital to replace his or her direct labor. This includes a belief in a classless society and in the capacity of every person to move up (or down) from the social position of their parents.

The myth is reinforced in numerous success stories found in the popular press. In these tales people beat pathways of commerce to the doors of the individuals and organizations who make better mousetraps. The myth is also institutionalized in the focus on "career" found in the schools. Special learning experiences are offered students, beginning in the elementary school, to help each person select the "track" which will help him or her realize the objectives of a better life through business.

Metaphor: Mechanism is the metaphor of capitalism. The economy is an engine of production which uses labor, capital and resources to grind out the products and services demanded by consumers. It is a machine which, if well-tended with appropriate inputs and control, has the ability to grow in pace with increases in population and human expectations.

This metaphor makes production the central concern of capitalist businesses and economies. Production results in jobs which enable individuals to improve their standard of living; its internal logic ensures the efficient use of scarce resources; its outputs benefit the entire society.

Model: The capitalist model is contained in the logic of production. It is one which tracks the flows of inputs and outputs at key points in the economic system. In its most general form, the model appears as the set of points and flows in Figure 2.2.

In this model, there are two principal actors (Firms and Households) and two markets (Factor and Product). Firms purchase the ingredients for production in Factor markets which results in Income for Households. This Income is apportioned to three flows (Taxes, Savings and Consumption). Consumption goes directly to Firms through Product Markets while Savings become the basis for Loans to Firms through the medium of Financial Institutions.

FIGURE 2.2

FLOW MODEL OF CAPITALIST ECONOMY

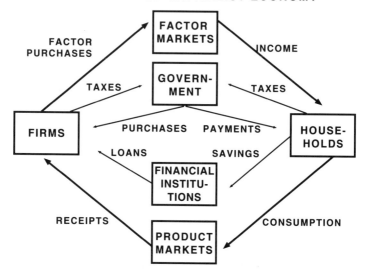

In this model, Government is a critical actor in that it collects Taxes from both Firms and Households. These revenues are used for various public purposes which result in Payments to Firms and Households for products and labor. In addition, Government Payments flow to these actors in the form of subsidies and welfare programs where there is no return of goods and services.

These flows result in efficient use of resources and maximum individual (Household) net benefit when they occur in an open, competitive marketplace. In that set of circumstances, all actors bid for products and services and all producers (Firms) attempt to maximize their market share through competitive pricing. In the long run, prices come to reflect the true costs of production and the relative values people set on its outputs.

The Paradigm of Communism

Mythology: The cornerstone of the communist myth is that labor is necessarily alienated from capital. The relations of production make it possible for capitalists to use the services of workers to create surplus value; this value enhances the power of the capitalist over workers and as Marx holds, the workers magnify the forces which dominate their lives (Marx, 1973).

The key message of this myth is that alienation is a necessary consequence of the relationship between labor and capital. If so-called "market forces" are allowed to structure the interaction of these players, labor will inevitably come up short. The net result is the class struggle which takes up so much space in Marxist economic writing and consumes the energy of so many *apparatchiki* in the socialist governments of the world.

Metaphor: The communist metaphor is a familiar one; it is that of the class struggle. This is economic warfare conducted according to political principles. It is, far and away, one of the most powerful metaphors in all of the social sciences. This is due to its comprehensive definition of all aspects of social relationships. No interests are outside its purview and few events escape its glib explanations.

While it's tempting to find the many weak points in Marxian economic theory, we are better advised to recognize the durable contribution of the metaphor of class struggle. This is the role of ideology in shaping economic and political action. For Marx, knowledge is under the control of those in power and it is used to further their ends. This concept has been applied with a particular vengeance as the communist class struggle has been carried worldwide. As ideology explains the economic and social circumstances of people and offers specific remedies, it is able to mobilize tremendous energies in the service of political objectives (Mannheim, 1936).

Model: The communist model is a simple one. It interposes Government in the flows of economic activity as the regulating mechanism.

Government is the arbiter of all decisions in this model. It decides what is to be produced and allocates the factors of production accordingly. Households provide their Labor as a general input to Government and there is no market mechanism whereby these inputs can be bid into new ventures or critically-needed activities. Producers receive targets from the central Plan and are held to these expectations by political control rather than market forces.

The same controls appear on the distribution side of this economy. Government controls the use of Outputs through a Rationing system. This is masked in most communist systems by set prices which give the illusion of availability of goods and services at fixed costs. In these economies, money is used as a social accounting device and not as the medium for communication between producers and households. Price has no larger meaning. This is evident in recent Soviet plans for price

FIGURE 2.3

FLOW MODEL OF COMMUNIST ECONOMY

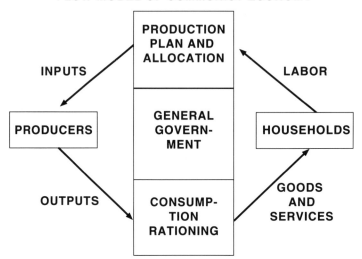

increases which are, in most cases, offset by adjustments in government-set wages.

The Case for a New Paradigm

Writing two decades ago, C. Wright Mills summarized the need for a new paradigm which could make sense of the emerging global condition of humanity.

> But what has been happening in the world makes evident, I believe, why the ideas of freedom and reason now so often seem so ambiguous in both the new capitalist and the communist societies of our time: why Marxism has so often become a dreary rhetoric of bureaucratic defense and abuse; and liberalism, a trivial and irrelevant way of masking social reality. The major developments of our time . . . can be correctly understood neither in terms of the liberal nor the Marxian interpretation of politics and culture. These ways of thought arose as guidelines to reflection about types of society which do not now exist. John Stuart Mill never examined the kinds of political economy now arising in the capitalist world. Karl Marx never analyzed the kinds of society now arising in the communist

bloc. And neither of them ever thought through the problems of the so-called underdeveloped countries in which seven out of ten men are trying to exist today. Now we confront new kinds of social structure which, in terms of 'modern' ideals, resist analysis in the liberal and in the socialist terms we have inherited (1959, p. 167).

Many business men and women would agree with Mills. The explanation and guidance offered by the capitalist and communist paradigms fall short when faced with the global problems summarized in Chapter 1. Their myths, metaphors and models do not provide the insights needed to chart the course of either business or public policy. Instead, we need a new paradigm, one which reorganizes our knowledge and experience so that we can address the issues of the nineties.

This new, Transformal Paradigm, is based on a world view of business activity where corporate and national boundaries give way to cultural and regional social systems. This is a view in which mythology is reflective of the potential of human knowledge and metaphors and models integrate business activity with social and physical surroundings.

Mythology: The mythical foundation of the Transformal Paradigm is the idea that information and knowledge are the primary resources for economic activity. This is a mythical idea in that it flies in the face of most commonly-held beliefs. There is also insufficient evidence to support the notion that economic use of information will improve the human condition.

On the other hand, there is a substantial segment of the business community which recognizes the increasing importance of knowledge as a resource. The beliefs of these actors are coming together to define a new view of economic organization in which the development, utilization and management of knowledge is central to business activity.

Metaphor: The central metaphor of the Transformal Paradigm is that of the knowledge worker. This is an individual who collects, analyzes and applies knowledge in pursuit of the corporate mission. In this metaphor, every economic flow is essentially information. Products are unique collections of knowledge; money is information about human needs and production potential; and the organization itself is a set of actors linked by information flows.

In a more restricted sense, the Transformal Metaphor is that of organization as "brain" (Morgan, 1989). As "brains" organizations are able to think, innovate and imagine new uses of knowledge. This unlocks human potential and directs all corporate resources at missions which transcend the narrow concerns of profit and loss.

Model: The Transformal Model is quite similar to the core model of the pure Capitalist Paradigm. It contains the basic flows of resources and income of that paradigm as shown in Figure 2.4.

FIGURE 2.4

FLOW MODEL OF TRANSFORMAL ECONOMY

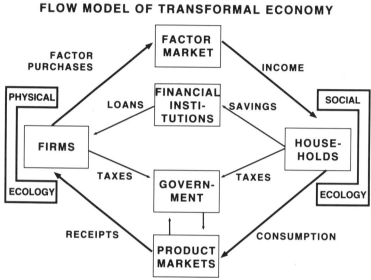

Where this model departs from its capitalist roots is in the economic function of government and in the model's emphasis on the ecological surroundings of economic activity.

Transformal governments continue to set the general rules for economic and social exchange. However, they do not engage in direct subsidies and services to Firms and Households. Instead, Government works within Product Markets to obtain its own needs and to provide services to citizens and organizations. As such, it distorts the market less than is the case in the capitalist model and it, too, is subject to the forces of the free market.

More importantly, the Transformal Model takes explicit account of ecology. First, it recognizes that Firms are set in a Physical Ecology where the question of renewable resources is of the first priority. By centering the attention of business men and women on ecological issues, it helps to ensure the long-range vitality of the economy. Second, the model positions Households in a Social Ecology. This makes it possible to consider the quality of life realized by Households and to take account of the effects of Income on it.

Paradigms in Conflict

These three paradigms are all in place to some extent in most cultures. There are adherents to communist and capitalist paradigms in virtually every country. There are also those who find these paradigms wanting and are actively searching for alternative perspectives on economic and social life. While those seeking change may not recognize the Transformal Paradigm as such, they employ many of its ingredients in the alternatives they propose.

In our next chapter, we discuss the process of paradigm change to show how conflicting points of view gain and lose their supporters. As we develop our analysis of paradigm change, we show how business organizations are affected by the myths, metaphors and models in the minds of their employees, managers and stockholders. This gives us a more detailed frame of reference whereby we can describe the ways our three paradigms structure the behavior of organizations and individuals.

References

Drucker, P. (1989) *The New Realities*. New York: Harper & Row.

Kuhn, T. (1970) *The Structure of Scientific Revolutions*. Chicago, IL: University of Chicago Press.

Mannheim, K. (1936) *Ideology and Utopia*. New York: Free Press.

Marx, K. (1973) *Grundrisse: Foundations of the Critique of Political Economy*. Harmondsworth, England: Penguin.

Mills, C.W. (1959) *The Sociological Imagination*. New York: Oxford.

Mooney, J. (1896) *The Ghost Dance Religion and the Sioux Outbreak of 1890*, 14th Annual Report of the Bureau of American Ethnology, Part II, Washington, D.C..

Morgan, G. (1989) *Images of Organization*. Newbury Park, CA: Sage.

Morita, A. (1990) *The Japan That Can Say No*.

Popper, F. and Popper, D. *The Buffalo Commons*.

Sterman, J. (1985) "The Growth of Knowledge," *Technological Forecasting and Social Change*, 28: 93–122.

CHAPTER 3

The Growth and Development
of Paradigms

Paradigm Definition

The paradigms we spoke of in Chapter 2 do not spring into being as fully-formed knowledge structures. Instead, they are created by people working on a specific set of problems which define the range of their interests. In the process of solving problems, these people accumulate a fund of information about effective ideas and practices. As this "fund" grows in size and scope, it begins to define a field where knowledge and application work hand in hand.

The integration of knowledge and practice is made possible by paradigms which both organize information and make it accessible to those involved in solving field problems. If this integration is to be effective, it must be based on what Thomas Kuhn calls "paradigm consensus," that is, a shared view of the field which helps practitioners choose solvable problems and assists them in accessing appropriate information (1970). Thus, in any mature field, there will be a single "ruling paradigm" which constitutes the basis for research and problem solving. If Kuhn's argument is correct—and there's a good deal of evidence that it is—then it should be possible to identify the "ruling paradigm" in any mature field.

We've taken the first step toward establishing the identity of business paradigms by suggesting that they are made up of myths, metaphors and models. This is a useful beginning, but it's not a very precise definition and it's not easily applied to the mountain of information accumulated by modern business organizations. We need, instead, a definition of paradigm which will enable us to deal with both economic systems and the sub-fields within business organizations.

Our response to this challenge is a view of paradigms as information-organizing structures. They are located in the exchange of information between the knowledge base of a field and practitioners (Ammentorp and

28

Johnson, 1989). The major features of this exchange are pictured in Figure 3.1.

FIGURE 3.1

PARADIGM DEVELOPMENT AND APPLICATION

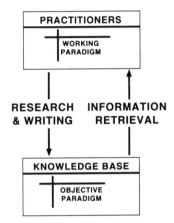

This approach is based on the assumption that knowledge must be organized in order to be used by practitioners. Specifically, the Knowledge Base of any field is indexed by a set of key words which are understood and used by all persons working on problems in that field. Since the knowledge bases of many fields are stored in computer data bases, it's relatively simple to identify the key words which are in current use. All we need to do is to examine a sample of records in the Knowledge Base and count the relative frequency of key words.

Those key words that are used most frequently are assumed to be important terms in the language of the field. They would, therefore, also be found in the myths, metaphors and models used by practitioners so that we can say "key words define paradigms." So far so good. But how exactly do paradigms emerge from this key word index system?

The answer to this question is found in the associations among keywords. As Practitioners use the Knowledge Base to solve problems, they will select those words which give them access to the information they need. Let's look at an example to see how this works.

Suppose a production manager is experiencing a high rate of failure of electrical components produced by a group of automated machines.

Upon examination of a sample of failed components, the manager decides that the problem is probably due to the settings of one or more of the machines. In order to solve the problem, the manager must be able to identify the specific machine(s) at fault.

As a first step, the manager decides to access the corporate quality control data base. This contains tools and techniques for using test results to identify causes of product failure. Since the data base is computer-managed, our manager is able to conduct a search of these tools/techniques using key words. The words selected by the manager are shown in Table 3.1

TABLE 3.1
PRODUCTION CONTROL
DATA BASE KEY WORDS

1) SAMPLING:	2) CONTROL:
Sample	Proportion of Failure
Size	Control Chart
Selection	Significance Test
Randomness	Error

This Table shows that the manager is drawing from two "knowledge clusters"; one related to the selection of samples of parts and the other to determining the significance of failures observed in the samples. These "clusters" are indexed by their associated key words and specific information within each "cluster" is accessed by the meanings of key words. Our manager has used the language of quality control to address the production problem.

The last sentence in the above paragraph gives us a clue as to the relationship between key words and paradigms. The key words our manager used were taken from the "language of quality control." They were useful keys to the corporate data base because they had special meanings within this "language." Let's push the example a little further.

The manager looks under the key word **sample** in the corporate data base. Under that heading, the manager finds instructions for creating a **sampling frame** which identifies each of the machines on the production line. The **sampling frame** dictates the source of **samples** which are taken using a **random process**. The **size** of the **sample** is determined by reference to **power curves** which help the manager control **sampling error.**

All of these "boldfaced words" are associated with one another. They are key words in a statistical model which enables users to calculate sample size and design sampling procedures. This model is at the center of the paradigm of statistical sampling theory which contains rules and procedures whereby sampling error can be minimized. By accessing this paradigm, our manager was able to take steps to be sure that sampling error was minimized in the quality control effort.

The statistical key words used by our manager assisted in solving the quality problem because they were terms in the rules of a model. The causal relationships in these rules told the manager what to do in order to attain certain objectives in the problem-solving process. Because key words play the same role in mature fields, we can identify paradigms and their constituent myths, metaphors and models by examining the occurrence of key words and their relationships with one another. This leads to the following definition of paradigm:

PARADIGMS AND THEIR CONSTITUENT MODELS ARE IDENTIFIED BY THE CO-OCCURRENCE OF KEY WORDS IN EITHER (A) GENERAL USE OR, (B) IN THE FIELD KNOWLEDGE BASE.

What this definition says is that key words occurring together in the same discussion, paper or article point to rules which can be used to solve problems. In our example, the association of the key words **sample**, **size** and **error** refer to a rule which states that the larger the **sample size**, the smaller the **error**. We show this definition in Figure 3.1 as two structures:

In these structures, the T-shaped lines refer to matrices where key words are listed on both horizontal and vertical dimensions and cells contain counts of the observed associations among key words in the paradigm. The Working Paradigm represents the ways Practitioners use key words while the Objective Paradigm refers to the ways key words are associated in the Knowledge Base. For a mature field, where there is a ruling paradigm, these two paradigms will be quite similar and there will be widespread use of the Knowledge Base in problem solving. For less well-organized fields, the paradigms might differ. In that case, Knowledge will not be readily accessed by Practitioners and the effectiveness of problem solving will be reduced.

Our definition has another feature in that it fosters paradigm growth and development. Referring again to Figure 3.1, we can see that Practitioners use Information Retrieval to access the Knowledge Base. Thus, Practitioners must know the key words and structure of the Objective Paradigm in order to tap the rules in its constituent model(s). As Practitioners experience problem solving success using the Objective Paradigm, they will bring the Working Paradigm into conformity with it. This will, over time, enhance the power of what will be the ruling paradigm as Practitioners add information to the Knowledge Base through Research and Writing.

We realize that some readers might find this discussion of paradigms somewhat abstract and that they may question its relevance for modern business practice. Our response to their concerns is that business men and women who wish to succeed in the information-rich environment of the nineties must have a clear and complete understanding of the processes pictured in Figure 3.1. There are no corporations able to conduct business as usual without making use of a large, rapidly-changing knowledge base. These businesses cannot use knowledge to design new products and services unless their Working Paradigms are congruent with the Objective Paradigms of the fields on which their activities are based.

There is a less obvious argument in favor of a paradigm focus in business. This has to do with the research and development activities of the business community as a whole. While each corporation wishes to keep its most useful knowledge secret from its competitors, there is a need to share basic knowledge to maintain the vitality of the Knowledge Base for the future. This is a new responsibility for many organizations and one which will be increasingly critical as regional and global competition increases in the nineties. What it adds up to is that corporations must be able to depend upon knowledge which they, themselves, help to generate.

Paradigm Evolution: The Case of Theory D

Another reason why business leaders must understand the paradigms of their fields is that they are continually changing. New knowledge and applications put old ideas to the test. When these ideas are found wanting, they call some aspect of the ruling paradigm into question. As researchers and practitioners answer these questions, they alter the paradigm so that its rules continue to be useful in the problem-solving process.

We can get a good idea of this process of paradigm development by taking a closer look at the quality control example discussed above. Problems of product quality have been one of the major concerns of production managers since the industrial revolution. Any complex production process is capable of turning out defective parts or assemblies and managers must be able to identify the cause of defects and take timely action in order to maintain profitability. This historical concern has resulted in a large knowledge base which has been structured around two interacting themes: Quality and Management.

FIGURE 3.2

THEORY D: THE EVOLUTION OF A PARADIGM

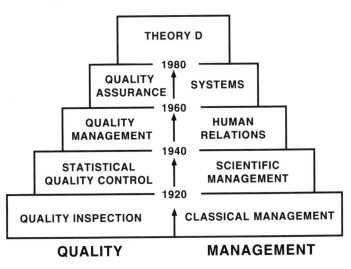

Over the past seventy years, these themes have evolved into a ruling paradigm for quality management—Theory D. This is a set of rules and principles whereby organizations can focus on the quality of products and services in an efficient manner (Deming, 1982). It grew out of Deming's work in Japan in the 50's and 60's where he created management systems which fostered organizational cultures in which quality was the guiding theme. It is a "ruling paradigm" due to its success as the organizational framework for Japanese production. When Edwards Deming began to work with Japanese business leaders in the 1950s, there were few who thought his emphasis on quality would have any effect on industrial products. After all, the Japanese had a world-wide reputation for producing junk. Everyone now knows that Deming was right; quality control and quality management worked for Japan so well that its products now constitute world standards of excellence.

Theory D is the summary of three decades of Deming's work in Japan. But, it's more than that. It's a paradigm for production management which is constructed on the broad foundation pictured in Figure 3.2. Each of the steps in that structure has had an effect on Theory D and, as such, illustrates the process of paradigm development in action. This is clearly evident in the ways the quality management paradigm changed in each of the twenty-year periods shown in Figure 3.2.

Pre–1920: In the early years of this century, managers believed that quality was "inspected into" products. Finished products were subject to standard appearance and performance tests by inspectors and the results used to pressure supervisors and workers for better performance. As a result, quality was an issue that got the attention of managers only when something was wrong; it was not a part of the day-to-day work of the organization.

This point of view was reinforced by the principles of Classical Management which held that each person in an organization had a well-defined function to perform. If everyone did his or her job, the organization would be a smoothly working machine. By compartmentalizing quality, this approach made it a punishing experience for everyone involved. And, it forced inspectors to enhance their position and authority by enforcing arbitrary quality standards.

1920–1940: Quality management paradigms began to take root during this period. The work of Shewhart (1939) and others at Bell Laboratories resulted in statistical models which incorporated basic measurement rules that rationalized the control of production processes. This gave quality control an objective foundation as well as a set of procedures which could be applied across the whole range of production operations.

At the same time, managers were focussing on the rational use of human resources in business organizations. This was the time of the Scientific Management movement when human inputs were entered into the production calculus of the organization (Taylor, 1947). In the quality control paradigm of the 1940s, it was possible to identify problems accurately and to compute the costs of both error and correction.

1940–1960: These two decades were a time when managers began to see quality control from a different perspective. It became an issue which crossed the boundaries of the organization so that the long-term reliability of products was seen as an indicator of quality. U.S. government specifications for maintainability of products played a significant role in this new point of view as they became translated into product design principles (Navy Department, 1972).

The expanded view of product quality went hand in hand with the so-called "human relations movement" in management thought. This movement made managers aware that the feelings and motivations of their employees had considerable influence on performance. As a result, managers were able to make improvements in product quality by paying closer attention to conditions of work, employee responsibility and fairness of compensation (McGregor, 1960).

1960–1980: The movement to Quality Assurance (QA) represented an expansion of quality models to include all stages of product development—from initial design through production, marketing and final use. QA is based on Juran's view that quality is "fitness for use" and that quality must be designed into a product if it is to be a durable property of value to the consumer (Juran and Gryna, 1980). QA also represents a systemic perspective on the design-production process. This expanded model helped managers to see that all decisions and activities associated with a product are part of a network of cause and effect. This is a network where managers can intervene at appropriate points to affect and assure product quality.

The systemic perspective of QA has a close parallel in the view of organizations as complex systems. Thus, there are models of organizational activity which focus management attention on causal networks which support design, production and marketing (Cleland and King, 1975). By 1980, there was a clear dominance of this systems paradigm in both QA and organization management and a more complete understanding of the impact of decisions on the work of the organization.

Theory D: What Deming does in his fourteen principles, is to collect the two strands of paradigm evolution shown in Figure 3.2 (1982). Despite the fact that it has been criticized as being "light" on its treatment of management (Mawhinney, 1986), it is extremely appealing due to its success in Japan. Theory D is a paradigm for production managers that cannot be neglected.

The power of Theory D is not only due to its demonstrated success. It is further strengthened by the fact that it builds on the key words used by several generations of quality control specialists and managers. Because the theory contains robust models and tested rules for applying them, it has all the ingredients of a quality management paradigm.

The evolution of Theory D also tells us that paradigms are closely related to problems. Theory D contains the models and rules needed to address problems having to do with product quality. It is cut to fit this class of problems. What this means is that other clusters of related problems have their associated paradigms so that we are likely to encounter paradigms large and small depending upon their focus and success. We can state this relationship in the form of another general principle: PARADIGMS ARE BOUNDED BY THE CLASSES OF PROBLEMS THEY ADDRESS. BY EXAMINING THE RULES AND MODELS USED FOR PROBLEM SOLVING, MANAGERS CAN ISOLATE THOSE PARADIGMS OF VALUE TO THE ORGANIZATION.

Paradigm Shifts: The Case of Perestroika

Paradigms are always in conflict. Any ruling set of metaphors and models has its competitors whose messages cry out for attention. This means that paradigms are always changing. They are adapting to new social and economic realities by giving us the tools to better understand our circumstances and to predict the consequences of our actions.

   These are paradigm shifts and they are generally so slowly paced that we are unaware of any changes in our systems of belief and action. Because these shifts are adaptive, they enable us to cope more effectively with our environment and we are gratified rather than disturbed by them. In fact, it's common for us to test our paradigms in order to identify the aspects of our models in need of modification. The results of these tests establish new patterns of cause and effect which strengthen the paradigm.

FIGURE 3.3

PERESTROIKA: Paradigm Modification

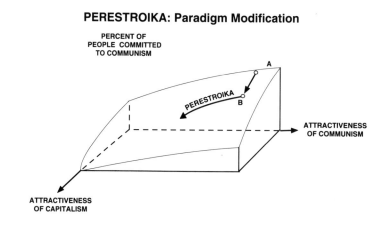

These paragraphs, we believe, summarize the underlying rationale for Perestroika as envisioned by President Gorbachev. The reasoning goes something like this: By subjecting the communist paradigm of social and economic organization to selected free market modifications, it would be possible to adapt that paradigm to a new global order. The surface shown in Figure 3.3 pictures the adaptations envisioned by Perestroika.

The forces requiring restructuring are shown as a tension between the "Attractiveness of Communism" and the "Attractiveness of Capitalism." For each point on the "Attractiveness" plane, there is a corresponding point on the "Commitment" surface. For example, in the USSR of the 1950s, the "Attractiveness of Capitalism" was at zero. Under these conditions, any increase in the "Attractiveness of Communism" would increase the "percent of People Committed to Communism." By the middle 1960s, it was probably safe to say that the level of "Commitment" was at the point marked "A" above.

As the Soviet Union moved into the 1970s, it became clear that capitalism could not be neglected. Increased economic relationships with Western nations began to show that there were attributes of capitalism that were essential to the economic well being of nations. These discoveries increased the "Attractiveness of Capitalism" so that there was some movement along the right-hand edge of the "Commitment" surface to the point marked "B" by the end of the 1970s.

It is to Gorbachev's credit that he recognized the need for adaptation of the communist paradigm and that any changes would probably lessen the total "Commitment to Communism" of the Soviet people. Remember, his sense of Perestroika included the possibility of alternative political parties that might represent alternative paradigms. This sort of planned adaptation of the Communist Paradigm is suggested by the arrow labelled "Perestroika" in Figure 3.3. The Soviet people would simply adjust their view of political economy to a new balance with some decline in the percentage of citizens committed to the communist paradigm.

As we have seen, the events of the late 1980s have discredited the hypothesis of smooth paradigm adaptation. Clearly the tension between the competing paradigms was at a level which would not permit the gradual change of the communist paradigm to some less doctrinaire version. The paradigm shifts in the Eastern Bloc nations were not the gradual changes of Figure 3.3. Instead, they were more like the catastrophic loss of Commitment shown in Figure 3.4.

FIGURE 3.4

KATACTPOfA: Paradigm Shift

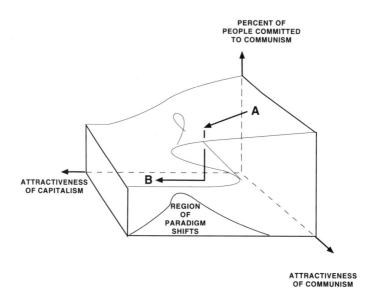

In this drawing, we are looking at the "Commitment surface" from another angle. From this perspective, we can see that the surface is folded and that, in the "Region of Paradigm Shifts" it's possible for drastic-catastrophic-changes in Commitment to take place.

This sort of folded surface is representative of what social scientists call a "cusp catastrophe" due to the shape of the "Region of Paradigm Shifts." It is a way of picturing social situations in which two competing forces can cause abrupt, or catastrophic, changes in belief and/or behavior (Woodcock and Davis, 1978).

In the case of Perestroika, the evidence suggests that the paradigm shift was something like the path sketched from point "A" to point "B" in Figure 3.4. By offering the opportunity for criticism of the Communist Paradigm, Gorbachev set in motion an adaptive process along the "Commitment" surface from point "A." Movement of Soviet opinion to the left along this line resulted in putting the Communist Paradigm at risk of a catastrophic loss of support. This is shown by the vertical line through the fold in Figure 3.4 which culminates in a new, lower level of Commitment to the Communist Paradigm at point "B."

This is not Perestroika (restructuring), it is Katactpoʈa (catastrophe). It is the sort of paradigm shift which occurs when policy-makers don't know where their constituents are on the "Commitment" surface. If they are anywhere near the "Region of Paradigm Shifts" there is a potential for Katactpoʈa. This is now history and communism has fallen into disfavor in the country of its birth. An opinion poll taken by Pravda in June of 1990 shows only an 18% level of support for the proposition that the communist system has the capacity to resolve the economic problems of the USSR (Pravda, June 23, 1990).

A critical feature of the model shown in Figure 3.4 is that any catastrophic change in Commitment cannot be directly reversed. That is, it's impossible to reverse directions along the vertical "catastrophe" line. Instead, Commitment must be carefully rebuilt by moving opinion around the "cusp" (Zeeman, 1977). Clearly, this can only be done by increasing the "Attractiveness of Communism." It cannot be accomplished by a return to ideological defense of the paradigm.

We can see this point in action in the current crisis of Lithuanian independence. When Soviet policy-makers removed ideological pressures from Eastern Bloc countries, they effectively permitted the "Attractiveness of Capitalism" to compete openly. This moved public opinion in those countries into the "Region of Paradigm Shifts" with the resulting Katactpoʈa. In the case of Lithuania, the Kremlin appears not to be willing to accept the political consequences of a loss of Commitment. Instead, there is an attempt to foster symbolic Commitment by using military force to support the Communist Paradigm.

Even though these actions are likely to prevail, they cannot move the Commitment of the Lithuanian people back to their pre-Katactpoʈa level of support for the Communist Paradigm. This is a powerful argument for the failure of ideology as a foundation for any paradigm. Once ideological underpinnings are removed, they cannot be reinstated. The failed paradigm can only recover by proving its validity in direct competition with the alternative perspective which caused its catastrophic loss of support.

Some General Principles of Paradigm Change

The above example can be extended to the general problem of paradigm change using several principles of catastrophe theory. These are:

1) Paradigm Shifts: These can be gradual without significant changes in the level of Commitment to the ruling paradigm except when there is

an unstable tension between the ruling paradigm and its major competitor. When that occurs, there may be catastrophic movements of Commitment from the ruling paradigm to its alternative. In the case of Theory D, we saw paradigm evolution in a non-competitive environment; in Perestroika, we see paradigm shifting under competition.

2) Irreversibility of Paradigm Shifts: When a catastrophic paradigm shift occurs, it cannot be reversed. Loss of Commitment to a ruling paradigm can only be recovered by rebuilding its attractiveness as compared to the appeal of its alternative. Thus, some modified version of communism will need to prove itself if it is to attract its former adherents. This principle is another demonstration of the importance of the paradigm's ability to solve problems. In effect, commitment to a paradigm depends upon its success (Kuhn, 1970).

3) Inaccessible Relative Attractiveness: There are certain balances of attractiveness between competing paradigms which cannot occur. These lie in the "Region of Paradigm Shifts" shown in Figure 3.4. Whenever relative attractiveness enters such a region, catastrophic changes in Commitment result. What this means is that changes in the problem-solving ability of a paradigm can move it to a point where its adherents lose confidence in it. When this happens, they are likely to seize on the alternative paradigm in order to reduce their uncertainty.

4) Divergence of Commitment: When the relative attractiveness of competing paradigms positions Commitment at the point of the cusp in Figure 3.4, small changes in attractiveness can move opinion to either the upper or lower levels of the "Commitment" surface. That is, small changes in the attractiveness of one of the competing paradigms can sway opinion in its favor.

5) Splitting Commitment: In the case of any ruling paradigm, there is a "normal" attraction due to its ability to solve problems. When it has a competitor, there is also a "splitting" attraction which transfers the loyalty of some to the competing paradigm. We see this in Figure 3.4 in that the "Attractiveness of Capitalism" can split many supporters of communism from adherence to its paradigm.

Implications of the Theory of Paradigm Change

The theory of paradigm change discussed above is more than an interesting way to describe management subject matter and political events. It can also be applied to social, religious and organizational paradigms to inform the strategies of leaders. The theory suggests several principles which can help to shape the process of paradigm evolution to avoid catastrophic change.

Abandon Ideology: Ideological support for a ruling paradigm places it at risk of catastrophic change. The corollary is that any worthwhile paradigm must stand the test of competition and must be measured by its capacity to solve problems and produce benefits for its adherents.

Example: One of the more familiar examples of a paradigm supported by ideology is that of the British Empire. The ideological position that the British system of law and government was independent of cultural forces placed the Empire paradigm at risk in many countries. When it proved unable to solve problems of economic development and ethnic conflict, it was catastrophically rejected in favor of nationalistic alternatives.

Examine Attractiveness: This is a matter of knowing the competition. The only way leaders can understand the issues in paradigm change is by knowing what attracts people to alternative points of view. Studies of this type can also result in knowledge about the strengths of the ruling paradigm which can be emphasized to enhance its competitive position.

Example: The Japanese management paradigm is probably the most significant alternative facing Western managers (Ouchi, 1981). This paradigm makes use of cybernetic self-regulating principles to focus the energies of workers on tasks and outcomes in a way not possible in Western corporations. By studying Japanese organizations, managers can better understand the competitive advantages offered by the alternative paradigm and make changes in their own organizations to make them more effective.

Adapt the Ruling Paradigm: In most instances, the ruling paradigm is a better choice. This is due to the fact that it has been built into organizational systems and into the language of its users. If it can be adapted, and its capacity to solve problems improved, it can better tap the energy of its followers than most alternatives.

Example: The American industrial experience with Just In Time (JIT) management is a case in point. Many corporations adopted this Japanese paradigm with the expectation that it would reduce inventory costs and increase adaptability of the production process. By overlooking some of its latent effects, such as new relationships with suppliers, employees and markets, users found JIT to be more disruptive than productive (Morgan, 1988). Those corporations which studied JIT and selected features likely to fit their existing organizational paradigm were able to avoid potentially catastrophic unanticipated consequences.

Paradigms and Organizations

The examples cited above make the point that paradigms affect organizations. They dictate how managers and employees view their work and they shape their patterns of behavior and interaction. In addition, paradigms contain the models of organizational processes which determine how inputs are to be transformed into products and services. In fact, there can be no organizations without paradigms.

In our next chapter, we address the paradigm-organization relationship to show how myths, metaphors and models structure organizational life. As a part of that discussion, we'll be attempting to make the case for a hierarchy of paradigms which tie the mundane concerns of production to the ecological environment of the organization. In this way, we hope to show that managers must pay attention to the problem-solving ability of high-level economic and political paradigms if their organizations are to remain viable in the 1990s.

References

Ammentorp, W. and Johnson, M. (1989) *Paradigm Consensus and the Organization of Scientific Literature.* Paper presented at American Educational Research Association annual meeting. San Francisco, CA.

Cleland, D. and King, W. (1975) *System Analysis and Project Management.* New York: McGraw Hill.

Deming, W. (1982) *Quality, Productivity and Competitive Position.* Cambridge, MA: Center for Advanced Engineering, Massachusetts Institute of Technology.

Gilbert, J. (1968) *A Manager's Guide to Quality and Reliability.* New York: J. Wiley.

Juran, J. and Gryna, F. (1980) *Quality Planning and Analysis.* New York: McGraw Hill (2nd. ed.).

Kuhn, T. (1970) *The Structure of Scientific Revolutions.* Chicago: University of Chicago Press.

Mawhinney, T. (1986) "OBM, SPC, and Theory D," *Journal of Organizational Behavior Management* (8).

McGregor, D. (1960) *The Human Side of Enterprise.* New York: McGraw Hill.

Morgan, G. (1988) *Riding the Waves of Change.* San Francisco, CA: Jossey Bass.

Ouchi, W. (1981) *Theory Z.* Reading, MA: Addison Wesley.

Shewhart, W. (1939) *Statistical Method from the Viewpoint of Quality Control.* Washington, DC: Graduate School, U.S. Department of Agriculture.

Taylor, F. (1947) *Scientific Management.* New York: Harper and Bros..

U.S. Navy (1972) "Maintainability Design Criteria Handbook for Design of Shipboard Electronic Equipment," Washington, DC: U.S. Department of the Navy, NAVSHIP 0967-312-8010.

Woodcock, A. and Davis, M. (1978) *Catastrophe Theory.* New York: E.P. Dutton.

Zeeman, E. (1977) *Catastrophe Theory, Selected Papers.* Reading, MA: Benjamin.

CHAPTER 4

Alternative Business Paradigms for the 1990s

Paradigms and Organizations

Paradigms are critically important for business leaders because they determine the shape of organizations and the behavior of those who work in them. We began our discussion of paradigms with this proposition and pictured the paradigm-behavior relationship in Figure 2.1. There, we suggested that paradigms define the social institutions which shape the relationships among people in a given culture. These include the rules of employment, contract, and authority which make organized activity possible. The most important of these rules are reinforced by political arrangements which bring the power of government to bear on economic life. From this foundation, business women and men gather resources and social support for their organizations.

The organizations they build will have a wide variety of missions. Some will provide services, others will produce products and some will attempt to influence social and political decision making. Despite the differences in mission, all organizations in a particular culture will reflect the underlying socioeconomic paradigm. Production organizations in communist countries will be characterized by employment and authority relationships drawn from the communist paradigm. Organizations with the same mission in capitalist countries will be quite different on these dimensions as they reflect the core myths, metaphors and models of the capitalist paradigm.

The bindings which tie business organizations to prevailing socioeconomic paradigms are extremely powerful. They are held in place by laws, administrative practices and by the beliefs of everyone who participates in organized activity. When the activities of organizations produce expected results, the underlying socioeconomic paradigm is reinforced and people believe in its mythology and have confidence in its models. If, however, results do not match expectations, there is a potential for paradigm shifts like those discussed in Chapter 3. These shifts can produce new paradigms which may or may not be closely related to older ways of thinking and organizing.

It is our contention that the events of the late 1980s have created a turbulent social and economic world environment where all existing paradigms are at risk of change. Communist paradigms have already been rejected politically in many countries and new organizational forms are being tested daily to find their replacements. At the same time, many features of the capitalist paradigm are being questioned in the hope that it can be shaped to address new global challenges. In these quests, business and political leaders are, for the first time, looking to social and economic results as the ultimate test of paradigm validity.

The centerpiece of our argument is that paradigms define business organizations and that any test of the utility of socioeconomic paradigms must take place in an organizational context. Thus, we need to be able to trace the effects of paradigms on organizations and to compare one with another in fairly specific terms. This can be done by asking the general question, "How do paradigms affect business organizations?" Our answer to this question takes the form of a table where the Communist, Capitalist and Transformal paradigms are arrayed against a set of basic organizational dimensions.

TABLE 4.1
ALTERNATIVE BUSINESS
PARADIGMS FOR THE 1990s

ORGANIZATION	ALTERNATIVE PARADIGMS		
DIMENSION	COMMUNIST	CAPITALIST	TRANSFORMAL
PURPOSE	Satisfaction of Needs	Standard of Living	Quality of Life
OWNERSHIP & CONTROL	State	Shareholders	Stakeholders
MODE OF ORGANIZATION	Bureaucracy	Corporation	Cybernetic
PERFORMANCE	Quotas	Profits	Value
DIRECTION	Administration	Management	Leadership
PRIMARY RESOURCES	Labor	Technology & Capital	Knowledge
DYNAMIC	Ideology	Entrepreneurship	Imagination

Table 4.1 shows that the impact of paradigms on business organizations can be measured along seven dimensions: Purpose, Ownership and Control, Mode of Organization, Performance, Direction, Primary Resources and Dynamic. These give us a frame of reference for comparing the effect of alternative business paradigms and help us to make a coherent case for the Transformal Paradigm.

Another message in Table 4.1 is that the Transformal Paradigm does not stand alone. It rests on human experience with both capitalism and communism and it draws on each to create new organizational arrangements which are more suited to the global business environment. Thus, we need to take a critical look at these historic paradigms to select what is useful for the world of the nineties. We need to approach the problem of global development with an open mind which in Pope John Paul's words, ". . . adopts a critical attitude toward both liberal capitalism and Marxist collectivism, for from the point of view of development the question naturally arises: In what way and to what extent are these two systems capable of changes and updating such as to favor or promote a true and integral development of individuals and peoples in modern society? In fact, these changes and updatings are urgent and essential for the cause of a development common to all" (1988, p. 648).

Taking this statement as our objective, let's look at each of the Dimensions in Table 4.1 to see what might be taken from our experiences with communism and capitalism and how our choices can be used as the roots of the Transformal Paradigm.

Purpose

ORGANIZATION	ALTERNATIVE PARADIGMS		
DIMENSION	COMMUNIST	CAPITALIST	TRANSFORMAL
PURPOSE	Satisfaction of Needs	Standard of Living	Quality of Life

In the past, any discussion of the Purpose of business organizations has tended in one of two directions. There has either been a narrow focus on Purpose as survival and profit or Purpose has been confused with the mission of specific organizations. These two points of view are both inadequate. Purpose refers to the role of business organizations in the larger society. It is responsive to the questions, "What are the benefits of economic activity and how are they distributed?" Purpose, therefore, must be calculated in the unambiguous language of costs and benefits and it must be weighed as to the ways these costs and benefits are shared by those who populate the business environment.

The importance of Purpose is clearly illustrated in the ways socioeconomic paradigms have been defended. Consider these two quotations:

(1) ... (capitalism) ... by the rapid improvements of all instruments of production, by the immensely facilitated means of communication, draws all nations, even the most barbarian, into civilization. The cheap prices of its commodities are the heavy artillery with which it batters down all Chinese walls, with which it forces the barbarians' intensely obstinate hatred of foreigners to capitulate ... (capitalism) ... during its rule of scarce one hundred years has created more massive and more colossal productive forces than have all preceding generations together.

(2) ... (the proper battle of government) ... is not just for equality as right and theory but equality as a fact and equality as a result.

The first of these quotations makes the point that the Purpose of economic organization is to produce those goods and services which will draw nations together as members of a civilized community. It argues that the record of capitalism makes it a powerful contender for the title of Most Useful Socioeconomic Paradigm. The second quotation looks at Purpose from a distributional perspective and sets a standard of "equality" which can be used to judge alternative business (and governmental) paradigms. This seems to give precedence to the communist objective of meeting the needs of all people through economic activity.

The interesting thing about these two quotations is that the first is attributable to Karl Marx (1904) and the second to Lyndon Johnson (1965). The father of communism extols the virtues of capitalism and the capitalist president endorses the objectives of communism! This is no chance paradox. Both Marx and Johnson are addressing the issues of Purpose: costs, benefits and distribution. In the texts from which these quotations were taken, it's also clear that both authors recognize that, "Good economics is not a 'zero-sum' game, taking from Petra to pay Paula. As a matter of fact, we may define good economics as policies that produce positive gains, even though victims may be created" (Buchholz, 1989, p. 280).

What does all this say about the potential contributions of capitalism and communism to a new business paradigm? First, although most of Marx's predictions concerning capitalism's exploitation of labor have been proven wrong, he has planted this issue firmly in the minds of many economic thinkers. Any paradigm must produce as low a level of misery as possible and must continually strive for improvement in the lives of all citizens. Communism also raises important issues concerning the ownership and control over productive resources. These concerns have given impetus to world-wide union movements and to various forms of worker participation in the direction of corporate affairs.

Second, capitalism has not only brought about the benefits cited by Marx and improvements in equality sought by Johnson, it has materially altered the relationship of people to their environment. It has been an engine of development whereby the standard of living of much of the world's population has been improved beyond imagination. It has also given rise to levels of compensation whereby workers have come to own ever-greater shares of productive resources through pension plan investment.

There are, of course, down sides to both paradigms. The communist system is one in which individual rights have no substantive meaning. Each person becomes a cog in a social machine which takes little account of his or her desires and no interest in matters of the spirit. It has also produced an unmanageable set of organizations which cannot respond to new ideas and challenges.

Capitalism, too, has its weaknesses. The most glaring is its capacity to gather the world's resources to use for the benefit of a few. This leads to the exploitation of the ecology with little concern for the future and to jealous defense of privilege. In short, capitalism wants for social and ecological conscience to channel its productive power. And, it can even blame the disadvantaged for social ills created by its own excesses (Ehrenreich, 1987).

Transformal Purpose can benefit from the goals of its capitalist and communist ancestors. By widening the scope of concern for the consequences of economic activity, the Transformal Paradigm can attempt to improve the Quality of Life of all persons. This means that the use of resources must be weighed against the long-run costs of depletion and pollution. It also implies that the benefits of economic activity must be distributed so that victimization is reduced and there is greater equality among participants.

This is fundamentally a case for an ecological perspective on business activity. Every business action has an impact on the physical and social ecology; a fact which business leaders must take into account in all decision making. As we will see in Chapter 5, this ecological perspective also has important political implications. It effectively sets new rules for economic games to level our playing fields so that all men and women have the opportunity to compete.

Ownership and Control

ORGANIZATION	ALTERNATIVE PARADIGMS		
DIMENSION	COMMUNIST	CAPITALIST	TRANSFORMAL
OWNERSHIP & CONTROL	State	Shareholders	Stakeholders

Ownership of resources and production organizations is the dimension where our three paradigms differ most significantly. In fact, it has been the distinguishing feature which has set communism and capitalism at odds throughout history. The reason it is so important is that Ownership and Control are two sides of the same coin. They give operational form to social and economic Purpose and, as a result, status and power to those who possess them.

There is a second reason why Ownership and Control are central to socioeconomic paradigms. This has to do with their use to create surplus value in the production process. This value is used to pay rents and interest on debt and to provide profit for owners. This is the fundamental argument of Marxist economic theory. Labor is employed by owners of the means of production in order that surplus value can be generated (Marx, 1976). Control over surplus value then alienates workers from their activities and widens the social distance between those who own the means of production and those who do not.

Communism seeks to redress the imbalance of benefit in society by changing the pattern of Ownership and Control. Its premise is that workers must own the means of production and that they must calculate and ensure their fair share of benefits before surplus value is put to more conventional uses (e.g. investment). The major problem with this premise is that "workers" are undefined and unorganized. Thus, the state must step in as a "surrogate worker" to exercise Ownership and Control in the name of "the workers."

The result of state Ownership is now clearly known to any reader of the popular press. It is rampant bureaucracy, inefficiency and overt exploitation of workers who have lost the Ownership of their labor in favor of secure assignment to a lifelong role in the production process. This leads to several disintegrative forces which make the Communist Paradigm an unsuitable base for global economic activity.

The most pressing of these forces is, in reality, an "anti-force." This is the bureaucratic stagnation of state-owned production systems. It appears as an inability to organize production to meet social needs. This stagnates growth and makes for unproductive use of resources. In the USSR, this "anti-force" has resulted in declining economic growth rates since the 1960s to virtually zero growth in the late 1980s (Khanin and Selyunin, 1987). It also shows up in the use of resources where communist systems can realize, at best, 40% of the return on production investments of the capitalist countries.

Even more critical is the attitude of workers within communist systems. This has been captured in the popular statement, "They pretend to pay us and we pretend to work." This attitude makes it impossible to produce quality outputs and we find that the solid communist goods of the sixties have been exchanged for worthless junk. It is no wonder that there have been catastrophic paradigm shifts in many of the Eastern Bloc countries.

The dismal performance of the Communist Paradigm makes for the easy argument that, "Instead of capitalism being a transition stage on the socialist road, it now increasingly appears that socialism is a detour on the capitalist road" (Drucker, 1989, p. 176). If this is, in fact, the case, shouldn't every business leader embrace the Capitalist Paradigm and continue the practices that have made it the winner in the paradigm wars?

There are many reasons why the answer to this question is "yes." They lie in the capacity of the Capitalist Paradigm to perform miracles of growth and deliver cornucopias of social benefit. These achievements have been made possible by patterns of Ownership and Control which allow individuals to generate surplus value for their personal use. Control makes it possible to profit by business activity and profit buys more Control and social power.

So long as the directions taken by owners result in increase in social benefit, capitalism has few effective critics. However, when those in Control lose sight of the social context of business, capitalist systems can be truly exploitive of people and resources. This is the major weakness of the Capitalist Paradigm; it has a narrow view of Ownership.

The Transformal Paradigm addresses this shortcoming head-on by shifting the locus of Control to those who have a stake in business activity. Under this paradigm, Ownership remains in the hands of stockholders who can expect to receive a return on their investments. They retain a controlling interest in the corporation, but it is modified by the interests of stakeholders. These are employees, customers, and others who are affected by the actions of the organization.

What this shift of Control does, is to keep business focussed on its social consequences. Under the Transformal Paradigm it is more difficult for business leaders to make short-run decisions which cause long-term harm to the social and physical ecology. In effect, the stakeholder concept accepts many of the social purposes of communism and uses the productive power of capitalism to make them a reality.

Mode of Organization

ORGANIZATION	ALTERNATIVE PARADIGMS		
DIMENSION	COMMUNIST	CAPITALIST	TRANSFORMAL
MODE OF ORGANIZATION	Bureaucracy	Corporation	Cybernetic

This dimension is used to describe the organizational arrangements whereby Control is exercised. Any complex organization must provide for the coordination of a wide range of activities which may be widely dispersed geographically. In order to do this, information must be collected, stored and channelled to decision makers so that appropriate action can be taken. When these information flows are linked to people, we find that a division of labor is created and that certain standard roles develop which cut across organizational boundaries.

These Modes of Organization vary depending upon the ruling business paradigm. Thus, communist organizations rely on Bureaucratic modes of operation, while capitalist businesses tend toward Corporate structures and practices. Each has its strengths and weaknesses as measured by its capacity to respond to problems created by turbulent business environments.

The communist Mode of Organization is mainly a modern version of traditional Bureaucracy. That is, it relies heavily on documentation and standard decision rules to coordinate business operations. It uses offices or positions as decision makers and arranges them in hierarchies of authority so that control can be exercised from a central location. In this Mode, no individual or group has a direct interest in performance; each is a functionary that acts much as a programmed decision maker to reach collective goals.

This is a Mode of Organization ideally suited to a static environment where pre-defined decision rules can be depended upon to work effectively. Since it discourages innovation and autonomy of action, it cannot respond quickly and accurately to turbulent environments. Consequently, it performs poorly in a global business environment. Centrally-defined objectives and decision rules are simply wrong by the time they reach the point of action.

Centralized bureaucracies are also notoriously poor users of human abilities. Because they emphasize collective attainment of goals rather than individual performance, they fail to motivate employees and managers. One result of this shortcoming is that low quality performance is the norm rather than an exception. Another outcome is that of collecting power through elaboration of detail. What this adds up to is organizations immobilized by control over the smallest detail where everyone's effort is directed at meeting targets set from on high.

The capitalist Mode of Organization also has roots in classical bureaucracy. It, too, uses documentation and decision rules to control business operations. However, there is a much greater degree of autonomy exercised by lower-level decision makers. This is Corporate organization where only general indicators of performance are centralized in the form of profit and loss. Lower-levels in these structures are free to pursue profit goals in whatever ways they think likely to succeed.

The strength of this Mode lies in the decentralization of bureaucracy. By locating decision-making authority closer to the organization-environment interface, Corporate organization creates the capacity to respond to environmental turbulence. It also unleashes individual creativity by making each person accountable for his or her contributions to the organization.

These attributes of the capitalist Mode of Organization are, paradoxically, the roots of its weakness. By decentralizing control, capitalism creates a competitive condition within the organization which can be detrimental to corporate goals and survival. In the extreme, each decision maker acts as an independent entrepreneur and is more likely than not to pursue his or her objectives at the expense of other members of the organization.

The Transformal Paradigm addresses the failings of Bureaucracy and Corporate Modes by treating the organization as a goal-seeking system existing within an environment. Goals are set at the boundaries where the organization interfaces with the environment. Inside these boundaries, the organization engaged in a variety of exchanges among units which are jointly controlled by individual decision makers.

The Transformal Organization is, consequently, concerned with flows of people, resources and product. And it is the task of decision makers to direct these flows to appropriate points in the organization where they can come together to maximize the value of the exchanges between organization and environment. This represents a true paradigm change where traditional bureaucratic concerns for *stocks* have given way to a systemic emphasis on *flows*.

We call this Cybernetic Organization to emphasize the role of information as the force which directs the activities of individuals and groups toward a collective goal. By using modern information technology, these Cybernetic systems increase the responsiveness of the organization to its environment. They also enable the organization to draw on the knowledge and skills of its members to resolve problems wherever they may occur.

Performance

ORGANIZATION	ALTERNATIVE PARADIGMS		
DIMENSION	COMMUNIST	CAPITALIST	TRANSFORMAL
PERFORMANCE	Quotas	Profits	Value

The Purposes we discussed above cannot be Controlled nor can they be Organized unless they are measured. Thus, every paradigm must provide for Performance indicators which can serve as benchmarks for business leaders. These are, of course, closely linked to the Purposes of organization and are, therefore, quite different across our three paradigms.

In the Communist Paradigm, Performance is measured in the form of Quotas set by central planners. The state Gosplan sets Quotas for each industrial, agricultural and mining sector. These become production and output targets which each firm, mine and farm is expected to meet. Targets are further distributed so that each organizational unit and work group has specific output requirements in front of it at all times.

At first glance, this seems quite sensible. If everyone meets his or her target, Quotas will be reached and the goals of the central plan will be realized. However, the threat of central punishment is such that targets are met by taking shortcuts that reduce the quality of outputs. It's not uncommon, for example, to see communist factory workers driving screws with hammers to meet targets. And, it's common to see substandard products which should not have passed even the most cursory quality control inspection.

The use of Quotas as a measure of Performance raises another, more fundamental, issue. Since centrally planned Quotas have no relationship to the wants and needs of people, there is no assurance that they result in desirable economic activity. When Quotas are coupled with the absence of a price system to prioritize production, we have a recipe for disastrous swings of emphasis which waste resources and destroy the confidence of citizens.

Capitalism attempts to avoid this pitfall by letting prices follow market forces. Thus, high prices are assigned to scarce, wanted goods and services so that producers are encouraged to make them available. If this mechanism works properly, the producer will be rewarded with Profits as a measure of Performance.

Again, if the relationship between price and social needs was perfect, the Capitalist Paradigm would be an effective base for economic activity. Unfortunately, there are, in most capitalist countries, forces which distort the free market. These forces are shaped by those who control the means of production and are wielded to enhance profitability despite social conditions. A case in point is found in U.S. agricultural policy where significant fractions of productive land are idled by subsidy payments in spite of the fact that many citizens want for basic nutrition.

By using Profit as a Performance measure, the capitalist system effectively de-emphasizes long-term goals. Managers must necessarily focus on short-run activities which will produce a better bottom line; they cannot afford to take a longer view without putting their careers at risk (O'Toole, 1983). The financial practices associated with a focus on Profit tend to subvert the basic work of the organization in favor of an emphasis on those activities which will enhance the trade price of its stock.

The Transformal Paradigm builds on the general idea of a free market. However, it shifts the Performance criterion to that of Value added by the organization. From this point of view, business activity must be reflected in the willingness of the market place to pay for it. What this means is that the quality of goods and services takes on first priority with managers.

Along with a focus on quality, the Transformal Paradigm encourages a longer view on the part of managers. Each becomes concerned with acquiring and maintaining market share through high quality goods and services. This does not mean that profitability is ignored; it means that profits are guaranteed over the long run by virtue of the Performance of the outputs of the organization.

Direction

ORGANIZATION	ALTERNATIVE PARADIGMS		
DIMENSION	COMMUNIST	CAPITALIST	TRANSFORMAL
DIRECTION	Administration	Management	Leadership

This dimension focuses our attention on the ways business leaders approach the task of coordinating and controlling the activities of the organization. Not surprisingly, each of our three paradigms encourages a specific view of Direction which is closely bound up with the Mode of Organization and the ways Performance is measured.

In the Communist Paradigm, Direction is Administrative. This means that persons in positions of authority make decisions and give orders in accord with pre-determined rules and standard operating procedures. There is no room for individual judgement in this form of Direction and, accordingly, little chance of error. If rules and procedures are well-chosen, organization activity can be easily coordinated. The task of the administrator in the Communist Paradigm is further simplified by the use of specific quotas and production formulae which guarantee their attainment.

The problem with Administrative Direction lies in the above "if clause." When the environment of the organization becomes turbulent, standard rules and procedures no longer work and administrators are unable to make innovative decisions. This binds the organization to the past and ensures that it cannot function in the global business environment.

Administrative directives also lock leaders in ritualistic behavior patterns. They become the *apparatchiki* whose power lies in position, procedure and rules. Access to these positions is not through merit. Instead, power is gained by seniority and adherence to the ruling paradigm.

By way of contrast, the Direction of organizations under the Capitalist Paradigm is Managerial in nature. The general Performance standard of profit gives managers considerable autonomy to set organizational Direction. It also enhances the responsiveness of the corporation, making it a more suitable Mode of Organization in turbulent times.

The effect of Managerial Direction on the individual business man or woman is also quite significant. There is an emphasis on merit and results which opens avenues of advancement to anyone with analytic and decision-making ability. Thus, it is possible for virtually any individual to advance in the corporate hierarchy by virtue of his or her Performance.

If there is a problem with Managerial Direction, it lies in the hierarchical nature of the corporation. Each manager is positioned in a ladder of authority which he or she cannot climb without a certain amount of conformity to the expectations of those at higher levels. This discourages risk taking and tends to focus managers on short-run Performance objectives. Thus, even though the Capitalist Paradigm makes for a more responsive organization, there is still a tendency to stagnation and organizational paralysis which runs counter to the needs of the times.

In the Transformal Paradigm, Direction is characterized by Leadership. This orientation differs from the managerial in that it fosters creativity and supports risk taking. The longer-range view of the Transformal Paradigm creates an organization culture in which experimentation and new ventures are possible. For the individual leader, this means that he or she is measured against a personal career path where advancement is acquired along with new knowledge and skill.

The Transformal Leader is one who arranges learning experiences for the organization (Bennis and Nanus, 1985). He or she is constantly in search of new metaphors and models which enhance the viability of the organization. This is a person who can make use of the knowledge Resource to assist the organization in gaining control of its exchanges with the environment.

Primary Resources

ORGANIZATION	ALTERNATIVE PARADIGMS		
DIMENSION	COMMUNIST	CAPITALIST	TRANSFORMAL
PRIMARY RESOURCES	Labor	Technology & Capital	Knowledge

As we turn to this portion of our table, it's important to note that each of our three paradigms makes use of all of the listed Resources. Each relies on some mixture of Labor, Capital, Technology and Knowledge to adapt organizations to business conditions. Where they differ, is in the relative emphasis given each Resource. These emphases reflect the way each paradigm views business problems and beliefs about the power of Resources to resolve them.

In the Communist Paradigm, Labor is the primary Resource for any business task and/or problem. By Directing Labor properly, administrators can bring a critical mass of skill to bear in each business situation. Somewhere in that mass, there are solutions to the needs of the moment. If that assumption is correct, concentration on the Labor Resource is quite appropriate.

The downside of the Labor focus is in its feudal perspective on production. Communist enterprises tend to be very large (there are only 700,000 enterprises in the USSR compared with more than 17 million in the U.S.) and have the appearance of feudal estates where workers are bound to the company store, housing, and human services (*Economist*, March 23, 1991). This makes for an undifferentiated mass of labor in which talent is masked in sheer numbers.

Organizations in the Capitalist Paradigm relegate Labor to a second place behind Capital and Technology. Mechanized, capital-intensive industry is the norm where routine work has been transferred from man to machine. Under stable market conditions and predictable inputs, this approach to Resource use is both efficient and effective.

It has, however, two weak points. First, by de-emphasizing labor, it tends to create a tension between workers and management. This leads, in the first place, to migration of enterprise to areas where cheap, willing labor exists. In the extreme, it results in replacement of labor by technology as in automation of production. Second, it fosters the belief that technology can solve all business problems. To the extent that this view prevails, it leads to waste of Resources, pollution and market disruption (Peet, 1987).

These problems are addressed in the Transformal Paradigm by shifting the Resource emphasis to Knowledge. This is not merely another word for technology. While it includes technical information, Knowledge casts a wider net to embrace social, economic and political information as well. In the Transformal Organization, Knowledge supports the continued evolution of organization metaphors and models and enables the organization to address problems which go beyond the bounds of traditional business.

The Knowledge Resource, unlike others, is renewable. Business organizations can add to their stock of knowledge by analyzing the results of their experiments and the transactions they have with their environments. This, more than anything else, is what makes the Knowledge Resource so central to the success of the Transformal Organization.

Dynamic

ORGANIZATION	ALTERNATIVE PARADIGMS		
DIMENSION	COMMUNIST	CAPITALIST	TRANSFORMAL
DYNAMIC	Ideology	Entrepreneurship	Imagination

The net effect of a business paradigm can be summarized in two statements. First, the paradigm fosters a view of business activity which shapes organizations and the behavior of those who work in them. Second, the paradigm generates a Dynamic force which drives individual performance and the expansion of economic activity. In a sense, everything comes together in the Dynamic associated with the paradigm.

The Dynamic of communism is Ideology. It is unquestioned belief in the tenets of communism and unswerving loyalty to the standard explanations of social and political reality. Ideology is based on the idea that socioeconomic relationships create patterns of thought which the individual cannot even perceive, much less adapt to new realities. Where the power of Ideology is most obvious is in the pat explanations and denunciations one finds in the communist press.

In closed societies, where everyone's thought and action is governed by a shared Ideology, there is no jarring discord between what one sees and thinks and reality. But, when such systems interact with people and organizations outside the communist paradigm, there are many events and conditions which cannot be explained Ideologically. When this occurs, Ideology and its paradigm are at risk of catastrophic loss of support. Since change is the defining characteristic of the global community, Ideology is a poor choice for a Dynamic to drive business into the future.

Capitalism has gotten round the limits of Ideology by resting its development on a different Dynamic; that of Entrepreneurship. This releases the individual business person from the bounds of ideology so that each can pursue organizational Purpose in his or her own way. It also energizes the individual in that benefits can flow directly from effort. In this way, Entrepreneurship is a powerful Dynamic which supports the growth of business activity.

The only failing of this Dynamic is that it tends to emphasize individual goals rather than those of the organization. In many instances, this results in the loss of talent as the Entrepreneur "takes off on his or her own." This is, of course, not totally unhealthy as the Dynamic exerts constant pressure on the organization in the direction of innovation and development.

The Transformal Dynamic is an extension of Entrepreneurship. It uses the creative Imagination of business men and women to define new Purposes and Models of Organization which are better positioned to meet environmental challenges. It is Imagination which takes a critical view of existing metaphors and models in order to shape them into new forms of business activity.

In effect, this Dynamic deals with images of organization (Morgan, 1986). It frees business leaders from traditional structures and processes and encourages them to make use of the Knowledge Resource in creative ways. Imagination is, consequently, the only viable Dynamic for the turbulent times ahead.

The Transformal Paradigm

The dimensions discussed above give a complete picture of business organizations along with some suggestions as to the ways paradigms affect behavior. In the chapters that follow, we will be taking a closer look at each dimension of the Transformal Paradigm. The purpose of this discussion is to identify some general principles which business leaders can use to transform their organizations to make them vital participants in the turbulent global business environment.

References

Bennis, W. and Nanus, B. (1985) *Leaders*. New York: Harper and Row.

Buchholz, T. (1989) *New Ideas from Dead Economists*. New York: Penguin.

Drucker, P. (1989) *The New Realities*. New York: Harper and Row.

Economist. March 23, 1991.

Ehrenreich, B. (1987) "The New Right Attack on Social Welfare," in F. Block, et.al., *The Mean Season*. New York: Pantheon Books.

Johnson, L. (1965) Quoted in L. Solomon and J. Heter, "Affirmative Action in High Education," *Notre Dame Lawyer*, 52(45) (October, 1976).

Marx, K. (1904) *A Contribution to the Critique of Political Economy*. trans. N. Stone Chicago: Charles Kerr.

Marx, K. (1976) *Capital*. New York: International Publishers, vol. 1.

O'Toole, J. (1982) *Innovation in Industry*. Paper presented at National Productivity Conference, Control Data Corporation, San Francisco, CA.

Peet, R. (1987) *International Capitalism and Industrial Restructuring*. Boston: Allen and Unwin.

Pope John Paul II. (1988) "On Social Concerns," *Origins,* vol. 18, 640-660.

CHAPTER 5

The Quality of Life

ORGANIZATION	ALTERNATIVE PARADIGMS		
DIMENSION	COMMUNIST	CAPITALIST	TRANSFORMAL
PURPOSE	Satisfaction of Needs	Standard of Living	Quality of Life

Every economic system has a Purpose which is understood by all participants. Purpose has to do with the effect of the system on the costs and benefits experienced by those involved in economic activity. Achievement of Purpose is, as a result, measured by the average value of this cost-benefit balance across all participants. This view of Purpose is based on the assumption that economic activity is distributive in nature and that no increase in benefits is possible without a corresponding increase in costs.

Thus, Communism seeks to Satisfy human Need by controlling all aspects of production and marketing. Similarly, Capitalism uses the discipline of free markets to enhance the Standard Of Living of its consumers and workers.

And, we contend, the Transformal Organization re-directs market forces in order to increase the Quality of Life of all people.

The achievement of these purposes involves the translation of national social values into a set of rules and guidelines which shape corporate policy. Through laws, administrative regulations and public budgets, governments send signals to businesses. These signals help business leaders decide what to produce, how to use human and material resources in production, and how to employ the profits of their business activity. Thus, any shift in Purpose toward Quality of Life requires a clear understanding of the associated social indicators and how Quality of Life might be expressed in measurable terms.

Social Policy and Business Practice

In our search for the impact of economic systems on the individual, we frequently assume that Purpose is a simple aggregate of individual wants and needs. We might, for example, emphasize individual needs for food, safety, income and, at the highest level, some form of self-actualization. These concerns are, of course, important to any society, but they can be misleading as criteria against which business practices might be judged.

The problem has to do with the costs of achieving these social purposes. Every nation has a finite amount of resources with which it can pursue its purposes. If these are in too short supply, purpose will be limited to more basic human needs of safety and survival. If they are more plentiful, they can become the focal point for political bargaining as powerful interests seek to maximize their share of benefits. Since purpose is evident, in the workings of both political and economic systems, it is very closely linked with symbolic values and public opinion.

The primary Purpose of any social system is the result of the common concerns of its citizens. These are articulated with government process and business activity through the media. In general, common perceptions of the attainable quality of life arise and each individual comes to believe that he or she should be able to access the amenities and opportunities portrayed by the media. Norms set in newsprint take shape in the visual impact of advertising and television and in the constant exhortations of radio.

We can see the media at work most clearly in developing nations where Western values are pictured in advertising and electronic media. It is probably accurate to state that the rising expectations of these nations is due mainly to the transistor radio and to culturally diverse representations of quality of life. Any small increment in quality of life anywhere in the world will, by virtue of international media, become an expecta-

FIGURE 5.1

THE ECONOMICS OF QUALITY OF LIFE

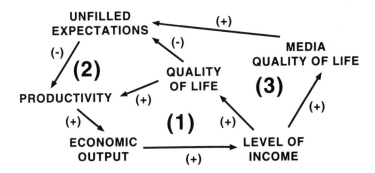

tion for nearly everyone else in the world. This makes it possible for something as mundane as designer jeans to sweep the world as well as ideas which foster fundamental changes in economic and political systems. It is no wonder that governments—especially unsuccessful ones—are so much concerned with media control.

The way this works is that media carries a composite picture—often in living color—of the good things in life. Any recipient of these messages can easily compare his or her own health, possessions, freedoms and opportunities against these images. This is a process which generates change through a network of relationships like that shown in Figure 5.1.

In this drawing, we show causality by the arrows and its direction by the plus (+) and minus (-) signs. A (+) sign on an arrow indicates that changes in the two variables are in the same direction. For instance, increases in Economic Output result in increases in Level of Income and conversely. Minus signs are used to show opposite changes; increases in Quality of Life lead to decreases in Unfilled Expectations and conversely. By following the pattern of signs through the network, we can see how any given variable brings about changes in all others in the network.

The central dynamic of Figure 5.1 is in the (1) loop which we might call a "quality of life generator." The way it works is that any increase in Economic Output leads to a corresponding increase in Level of Income. This, in turn, results in improvements in Quality of Life and to greater Productivity on the part of those involved in economic activity. As the loop is completed, these Productivity improvements are translated into a growing Economic Output and the set of relationships is set for another round of cause and effect.

This "quality of life generator" is what gives capitalism the edge over other economic systems. There are many instances where the "generator" has led to astonishing improvements in Quality of Life. Consider the following analysis of the gains in Quality of Life made by residents of Korea and Taiwan. "A Taiwanese child born in 1988 could expect to live 74 years, only a year less than an American or a West German and 15 years longer than a Taiwanese born in 1952; a South Korean born in 1988 could expect 70 years on Earth, up from 58 in 1965. In 1988, the Taiwanese took in 50% more calories each day than they had done 35 years earlier. They had 100 times as many televisions, telephones and cars per household; in Korea the rise in the possession of these goods was even sharper. Virtually all Taiwanese and Koreans go through elementary school and 45% of Taiwanese and 37% of Koreans get at least some

higher education (like 60% of Americans, but only 22% of Britons). ...
Taiwan's unemployment rate was 1% in 1988; the last time it exceeded
2% was 1964. Korea's rate has hovered between 2% and 4% for all but
one of the past 20 years ... . And, ... for much of the past two decades,
Taiwan has been the world's most egalitarian society as well as one of
the half-dozen fastest growing ones" (*The Economist*, July 14, 1990).
Clearly, the "generator" works.

However, the "generator" does not stand alone. It is influenced by the
perceptions of citizens and workers. This is what we call the "productivity control loop" (2) in Figure 5.1. Each person has an expectation of what
his or her Quality of Life ought to be. That is, any increase in Quality of
Life leads to a reduction in Unfilled Expectations. These reductions are
passed along as increases in Productivity, due to the (-) sign on the linking arrow. As long as Quality of Life meets expectations, the "generator"
loop can work and we can experience growth in Economic Output and
increases in Quality of Life (Rice, et.al., 1985).

If Expectations remained static, any increase in Output or Quality of
Life would set the "generator" at work to produce a spiral of growth and
well-being. But media enters the picture by creating a vision of quality of
life (Media Quality of Life) which is an idealized version of reality. This
is the "expectation-raising loop" (3) which distorts the current Level of
Income into images of Quality of Life that cannot be attained by any but
a small number of people. This distortion leads to increases in Unfilled
Expectations and to decreases in Productivity. As these decreases work
their way through the network, they ultimately affect Quality of Life to
make matters even worse.

The dynamics of this network are particularly significant for developing nations where media are heavily conditioned by Western values. Citizens in developing nations are subject to representations of Quality of
Life which cannot be sustained by prevailing levels of Economic Output.
People in these countries perceive that modern urban life is associated
with quantum leaps in Quality of Life and Expectations soar only to
break against the reality of limited opportunity. This is especially true for
nations which suffer from the joint pressures of population growth and
resource scarcity; where gains in Output are speedily consumed by the
costs of maintaining a static, if not actually decaying, Quality of Life.

These issues are important for business leaders as there is growing public concern for the Quality of Life in all nations. There is an emerging
awareness of the global problems we discussed in Chapter 1 and increased
political pressures for basic Quality of Life guarantees. What this all

means is that governments are enacting mandates which establish mini-mum standards of access, opportunity and environment for all citizens.

These pronouncements take various forms. On the one hand, there are the legal guarantees which support business transactions; laws concerning product liability, contracts, and restricted practices. On the other, there is a trend in many Western nations toward more wide-ranging specifications of the quality of customer/client experiences. An example of this trend is the recent enactment in the U.S. of federal regulations containing specific mandates as to the quality of life and quality of care in nursing homes (Ammentorp, et.al., 1990). What these initiatives tell us is that Quality of Life is among the major political issues of the 1990s. They also speak directly to business women and men in that economic activity is the means whereby quality goals are met.

Quality of Life: A Warm Fuzzy? or Just a Fuzzy?

In borrowing this heading from our treatment of quality in the human services, we are recognizing a fundamental problem with Quality of Life (Ammentorp, et.al., ibid). It is a "fuzzy" concept; one which leaves lots of room for individual definition and political bargaining. Nevertheless, as Quality of Life becomes more widely debated and governments test legal guarantees of quality, there is a developing consensus as to what makes for a quality living experience. Because so much hinges on this shared view of Quality of Life, it is imperative that business leaders dispel some of the fuzziness that may surround the notion of quality in their own minds. The best way to do this is to consider how Quality of Life has been treated in the large by governments and national consumer groups as well as how it has been dealt with in the small by individual citizens.

Despite the recency of Quality of Life legislation, there has been a long history of concern for the living experiences of citizens. This can be traced to the so-called "social indicator movement" of the 1960s in which policy analysts attempted to determine whether public expenditures resulted in Quality of Life improvements. This "movement" attempted to create broad-based indicators which would permit the computation of a Gross Social Product—much like GNP—to inform policy decisions.

The search for social indicators can be traced to the federal programs of the 1930s. These programs were enacted in the hope that they could ameliorate the social disorganization of economic depression. To assess their impact, the U.S. president formed a Committee on Social Trends which reported on the Quality of Life in America (Ogburn, 1933). The report, however, lay dormant until the technological developments of the fifties and sixties raised the question of impact of governmental programs on employment and Quality of Life.

In the late 1950s, the National Aeronautics and Space Administration set out to identify the "second order" consequences of investment in space technology. NASA commissioned the American Academy of Arts and Sciences to assess the impact of technology and to identify ways to anticipate the social changes occasioned by technological policy. The resulting report of the Academy's study, *Social Indicators*, was published in 1966 (Bauer, 1966). The key concept in the report is summarized by Bauer as, ". . . the problem of measuring the impact of a single program could not be dealt with except in the context of the entire set of social indicators used in our society." (p. 1) This was addressed in *Social Indicators* in a major paper by Gross in which a set of social accounts was proposed. These were to be continually monitored to examine the network of consequences following on any specific technological initiative. (ibid, 154–271)

This idea is captured in the following definition, "A social indicator may be defined to be a statistic of direct normative interest which facilitates concise, comprehensive and balanced judgements about the conditions of major aspects of a society. It is in all cases a direct measure of welfare and is subject to the interpretation that, if it increases in the 'right' direction, while other things remain equal, things have gotten better or people are 'better off.' Thus, statistics on the number of doctors or policemen could not be social indicators, whereas figures on health and crime rates could be" (Olson, 1969, p. 7).

These ideas are at the root of current international perspectives on Quality of Life. When the United Nations files its annual report on the condition of children across the world, it focuses attention on such indicators as infant mortality and nutrition (United Nations, 1988). These statistics form a basis for evaluating the effects of national policy and developmental status on the living experiences of children.

Social indicators also make it possible to form a rough rank order of nations as to the Quality of Life they offer their citizens. In Table 5.1, we show the top and bottom five nations ranked according to a "human development index" devised by the United Nations Development Program (United Nations, 1990). This index is a combination of three social indicators: the level of adult literacy, life expectancy and per-capita purchasing power.

TABLE 5.1
NATIONAL RANKING OF
HUMAN DEVELOPMENT

COUNTRY	LIFE EXPECTANCY	ADULT LITERACY	PURCHASING POWER	HDI
Top Five:				
Japan	78	99	$13,135	.996
Sweden	77	99	13,780	.987
Switzerland	77	99	15,403	.986
Holland	77	99	12,661	.984
Canada	77	99	16,375	.983
Bottom Five:				
Niger	45	14	452	.116
Mali	45	17	543	.143
BurkinaFaso	48	14	500	.150
SierraLeone	42	30	480	.150
Chad	46	26	400	.157

While these rankings are similar to those resulting from the use of Gross National Product statistics, they differ in that they allow for factors which are more directly related to Quality of Life. First, the use of life expectancy factors health and nutrition into the quality equation. Second, literacy measures the extent to which all citizens have access to opportunity. Finally, the use of purchasing power compensates for the relative prices of goods and services.

Rankings of this type raise the question, "What are the economic conditions and social policies which set these nations apart?" Clearly economic systems make a difference. No communist country is among the top twenty in the human development ranking. Political priorities also count. Those countries at the bottom of the above ranking are those that spend an inordinate fraction of national income for military purposes; Japan has 25 soldiers for every 100 teachers while Somalia (seventh from the bottom) has 525/100. The conclusion is clear; by enhancing economic development and limiting military expenditures, nations can improve Quality of Life. There can be little debate on this point.

The data, however, hide another aspect of political life. That is the exploitation of the disadvantaged by those with political and economic power. For example, in Zimbabwe (ranked 52 from the bottom—of 130 nations), 4,000 whites own the best one-half of the land while 4,000,000 blacks exist on the poorest one-half. Thus, Quality of Life is not only development. It is re-structuring of the relationships among people; a levelling of opportunity; and a promotion of the dignity of all people.

This is not a "warm fuzzy." This is social reality and must be addressed in the nineties in order to limit social disorganization and catastrophic migrations. It is also a global imperative which politicians and business leaders neglect at their own peril. We have already seen how glimpses of opportunity have shaken the foundations of communist social and economic systems. What we all must realize is that our own foundations are nearly as shaky when built on underpinnings of human misery.

These realities can be effectively managed only by focussing on a "true development" which ". . . is in keeping with the specific needs of human beings—man or woman, child, or old person—. . . (and which). . . implies, especially for those who actively share in the process and are responsible for it, a lively awareness of the value and rights of all and of each person. It likewise implies a lively awareness of the need to respect the right of every individual to the full use of the benefits offered by science and technology" (Pope John Paul, 1988). This is a clear call to a recognition of the benefits created by economic activity and to the ways social and political systems distribute them to people. It is a recognition of social justice as the cornerstone of Quality of Life. This point of view can be summarized as a "commandment." "Recognize that social and economic justice are one and the same and that each person has the right to participate fully in the economic systems which dictate his or her life chances" (DeThomasis, 1989, p. 21).

Toward a Corporate Social Agenda

Once business leaders have accepted the over-riding importance of Quality of Life, they can shape corporate missions to improve access to the benefits they create. This can be reduced to a two-part Social Agenda. First, corporations must create benefits in ways which preserve the ecological relationship between humankind and its environment. Second, corporate missions must be sensitive to the distribution of benefits and to their effect on Quality of Life. These are, obviously, cosmic issues which haven't, up to this point, received much attention. They are, however, issues which every corporation must grasp to ensure its own survival in a global society which is increasingly conscious of their central importance.

The Corporate Ecological Mission: This is by far the easier of the two issues for business leaders. It is based on the principle that every corporation has an impact on the surrounding ecology. It uses resources to do its work and deliver its products and services—along with their unintended consequences. The sum total of these exchanges must add up to a positive impact on the ecology if the corporation is to have a useful social agenda.

The effects of economic activity on global ecology are clearly articulated in recent studies (Business Week, 1990). The spread of greenhouse gases and industrial pollution can be directly traced to the shortcomings of corporate policy. Tropical deforestation is driven by the economics of resource exploitation. Poor resource management has led to depletion of groundwater, soil erosion and the diminution of virtually every finite resource. These are very real costs which business women and men must factor into their balance sheets if their records are to reflect the long-term viability of the corporation.

Put another way, if corporations are to engage in ecological damage control, they will not only need policies which give lip service to the above issues. They will also need a change in the internal standards whereby employee and managerial performance is evaluated. The narrow, short-range concerns for quarterly profits will need to be replaced with a longer-range view of corporate viability and the "fit" between the corporation and its ecology.

For example, the current issue concerning the balance between timber cutting and owls in the American Northwest must be evaluated in the long term. To say that timber must be cut to produce short-run profit and local jobs is to neglect the facts of economic life. When the timber is gone, there will be no jobs and a slowly-renewable resource will have been squandered for fleeting benefits. The clear mandate for the corporation is to continually revise its policy of sustained production to maintain a working ecological balance. If this involves income short-falls or changes in employment, the corporation will need to balance these against its long-run vitality. This does not mean that owls take precedence over people; they are only a signal of the impact of people on environment and their call cannot go unheeded.

Corporate Mission and Quality of Life: This is by far the more difficult of the two mission-related issues raised above. The reason it is so difficult is that there are often profits to be made by goods and services which detract from the Quality of Life. For instance, it is profitable for many corporations to be involved in the production and trade of weapons. Corporations have argued that weapons are essential to keeping the peace in the world and "somebody has to do it." There is the additional justification that "guns don't kill people, people do."

At this stage of history, it should be clear to everyone that these "bumper sticker" slogans are false. Armaments destabilize the world and diminish the Quality of Life and add to the misery of countless millions of people.

They also distribute the means of violence so widely that aggressive behavior can no longer be controlled in the political exchanges of nation states. Instead, each group and many individuals have the capacity to destroy thousands and to escape detection in the process.

What this example tells us is that the corporation is responsible for the human consequences of its actions. When a pistol made in Massachusetts kills a banker in Germany, the manufacturer and those in the distribution chain all have a share in the act. Goods and services are not neutral; they have social impact through the ways customers put them to use. Consequently, the corporation must look to the minds of its customers to determine whether its output adds to the global Quality of Life.

This is the crux of the matter. Many corporations which profit by reducing the Quality of Life will need to transform themselves to a new level of social responsibility. For many, this will mean new products, new customers, and the risks that go along with a new business territory.

How is this to be done? The only way the corporation can transform its mission is to have a clear understanding of its relationships with its surrounding ecology. This necessarily involves detailed models of the resource flows and ecological impact of business which permit accurate calculation of the costs of its activity. It also includes a thoughtful analysis of the social benefits the corporation delivers; an analysis which must incorporate both negative and positive effects of goods and services (Hohn, 1982). By putting its relationships with the ecology on an analytical plane, the corporation is taking the necessary steps to transform itself into a force which supports global Quality of Life.

The Quality of Worklife

Quality of Life issues are not limited to the ecological relationships of the corporation. They extend to its innermost workings where the quality of experience of employees comes into play. In Figure 5.1, we suggested that Quality of Life had a direct effect on Productivity. In the above paragraphs, we treated this relationship as a general social consequence of Economic Output. It has, however, a more basic meaning which has to do with the ways the work experience is translated into productive behavior by employees.

This Quality of Life issue is also two-fold; it rests on the relationship between the worker and his or her firm, under the constant pressure toward high-technology, information-based work. To ensure a quality work experience under these conditions, the corporation must adopt a new perspective on human resources—one which breaks down the traditional tensions between white-and bluecollar workers. As a recent study group has noted, "Most U.S. firms are divided into a two-class society: Research, design, finance, and sales people are first-class human beings; production people are second class. . . . (CEO's agree) . . . that this two-tiered corporate society is often detrimental to developing and producing new and/or improved products" (Harris Bank, 1990).

The effects of the traditional social structure of the firm on productivity calls for a new paradigm. This is one which assigns equal importance to the contribution of all workers. It is also one which is much concerned with the meaning of work so that employees see that their activities "add up" to goods and services of value. This means that the paradigm must run counter to the "abstraction of work" which distances people from what they do and makes them one other standardized production input (Zuboff, 1988).

In the Transformal Paradigm, Quality of Worklife is determined by the ways the organization designs and manages social and technical activities (Herbst, 1974). The work of any organization is directed by the technology it uses to convert resources to products and/or services. Each technology sets specific requirements as to what workers must do and how they must interact with one another. Left alone, these requirements create rigid, sterile environments where work is "abstracted" and has no meaning. In order to overcome the debilitating impact of technology on the worker, managers must direct their attention to the social aspects of life in the organization.

In Transformal Organizations, this is done by looking to the behavior of managers and employees so that each person's activities can be suitably reinforced by the natural flow of work (Luthans and Kreitner, 1985). Through careful design of the socio-technical aspects of organization, managers can create an environment which elicits the loyalty of employees and maximizes their productivity.

A Transformal View of Quality of Life

The quality issues outlined above appear as the centerpiece of the Transformal Paradigm. They are the root concerns of managers and business leaders as they determine the productive efficiency of the organization and the social value of its outputs. By taking an ecological perspective on the relationship of the organization to its surroundings, the paradigm ensures that the daily exchanges between organization and environment will result in a better "fit" between the two. As managers use this perspective to direct the internal affairs of the organization, there will also be a good "fit" between employees and the organization. In Figure 5.2, we show these "fits" as Quality targets.

FIGURE 5.2

ORGANIZATION AND ECOLOGY:
THE QUALITY CONNECTION

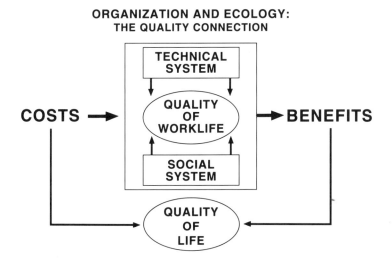

Here, Quality of Worklife represents the "fit" of individuals to the organization. As noted above, it is the resultant of the ways the individual experiences the Social and Technical Systems in the organization. To the extent that managers are able to create a quality work experience, employees will be both satisfied and productive. This will make the organization able to produce a significant flow of Benefits at relatively low Cost.

This Cost-Benefit balance appears in the larger society in the form of organizational contributions to Quality of Life. While no single organization has a significant impact on the over-all global or national Quality of Life, it must add to the balance of Benefits over Costs if it is to survive and prosper. Organizations with excessive Costs will fail and those with a marginal Cost-Benefit balance are at risk. The Transformal Leader has these balances at his or her fingertips; he or she creates a Quality Work-life which continues to improve the social relevance of the organization.

In the chapters ahead, we will address the management issues raised by this Paradigm in greater detail. Throughout these discussions, the central theme is that of "ecological fit" and the management task that of making decisions which will enrich human experience. In doing this, we are adding a moral dimension to management; one which is designed to ". . . stir the conscience of the . . . (business). . . community to become involved, in a spirit of liberating change, with the burning social, political and economic issues facing the world at this critical juncture in its history" (Lane, 1984, p. 139).

References

Abbey, A. and Andrews, F. (1985) "Modeling the Psychological Determinants of Life Quality," *Social Indicators Research*, 16, 1–34.

Ammentorp, W., et.al. (1990) *Quality Assurance for Long Term Care Providers*. Newbury Park, CA: Sage.

Andrews, F. and Withey, S. (1976) *Social Indicators of Well-Being*. New York: Plenum Press.

Bauer, R. (1966) *Social Indicators*.

Campbell, A. (1981) *The Sense of Well-Being in America*. New York: McGraw Hill.

Davis, L. and Cherns, A. *(1975) The Quality of Working Life*. New York: Free Press.

DeThomasis, L. (1989) *Monastaries on Wall Street: The Ten Commandments of Doing Ethics in Business*. Winona, MN: St. Mary's College.

Harris Bank (1990) *Conversations for the 90's*. Chicago IL: Harris Trust and Savings Bank.

Herbst, P. (1974) *Socio-Technical Design*. London: Tavistock.

Hohn, S. (1982) "Economic Development and Ecological Equilibrium: A Target Conflict in Modern Industrial Enterprises," *Long Range Planning* 15(4), 22–36.

Landesman, S. (1986) "Quality of Life and Personal Life Satisfaction," *Mental Retardation*, 24(3), 141–143.

Lane, D. (1984) *Foundations for a Social Theology*. New York: Paulist Press.

Luthans, F. and Kreitner, R. (1985) *Organizational Behavior Modification and Beyond*. Glenview, IL: Scott, Foresman.

Ogburn, W. (1933) *Recent Social Trends.*

Olson, M. (1969) *Toward a Social Report.*

Pope John Paul II (1988) "Solicitude Rei Socialis," *National Catholic Reporter*, 24(31), p. 13.

Rice, R., et.al. (1985) "Organization Work and the Perceived Quality of Life," *Academy of Management Journal* 16(2), 296–310.

"Taiwan and Korea: Two Paths to Prosperity," *The Economist,* July 14, 1990, pp. 19–22.

United Nations (1988) *The World's Children.* Geneva, SW: United Nations.

United Nations Development Program (1990) *Human Development Report 1990.* Geneva, SW: United Nations.

Zuboff, S. (1988) *In the Age of the Smart Machine: The Future of Work and Power.* New York: Basic Books. 24(31), p. 13.

Rice, R., et.al. (1985) *"Organization Work and the Perceived Quality of Life,"* Academy of Management Journal 16(2), 296–310.

CHAPTER 6

Stakeholders in the Transformal Organization

ORGANIZATION DIMENSION	ALTERNATIVE PARADIGMS		
	COMMUNIST	CAPITALIST	TRANSFORMAL
OWNERSHIP & CONTROL	State	Shareholders	Stakeholders

It's impossible to talk about the purpose of business organizations without addressing the issue of Ownership and Control. In order to pursue corporate goals, decisions need to be made and resources allocated to specific objectives. These decisions are invariably made from a power base founded on the ownership of corporate assets and no organization is possible without a clear delineation of the link between resources and purpose.

In the Communist Paradigm, all organizations are creatures of the State. It owns all assets and has complete control over the day-to-day workings of organizations. As a result, the Purpose of economic organizations is always closely bound up with political goals and all economic activity is directed at strengthening the State. As we've seen recently, this leads to organizational paralysis and the inability to accommodate change.

The Capitalist Paradigm brings Purpose and Ownership together in the individual firm. This makes it possible for firms to respond to new circumstances which is all to the good. However, it also reinforces narrow pursuit of individual Shareholder interest. This has, over time, led to an approach to Control which emphasizes the financial goals of Shareholders over the business objectives of the organization. While such an approach can maximize the gains of Shareholders, it generally does not ensure the vitality of the corporation; in the extreme, it can lead to "break up" of the firm for short-run profits.

These two traditional paradigms are both inadequate to the business environment of the nineties. Their goals are incompatible with an ecological view of organization and their Control practices stand in the way of the decisions which must be made in response to the demands of the global economy. In their place, businesses need a comprehensive view of Stakeholders and a means to transform their interests into sound corporate objectives.

Pursuing Corporate Goals

The achievement of the quality of life mandate we've set for business in the nineties is the responsibility of those who care for the assets of the corporation. These are Stakeholders and they have a special interest in the health of the organization and the nature of its products and services. Theirs is a long-range view which emphasizes the "fit" between the corporation and its ecology. The actions they take are directed at shaping the interactions between the organization and its environment to better accommodate social and economic change. As Alkhafaji puts it, "Society expects that corporations will meet its needs, values, and interests. It also expects the corporation to maintain control over its decision making so as to minimize the externalities (e.g. pollution) and assume greater accountability to correct social ills . . ." (1989, p. 36).

The perspective of Stakeholders is in marked contrast to that of Shareholders in the Capitalist Paradigm. The goal of the Shareholder is to maximize the short-run return on his or her investments. Accordingly, their behavior centers on the ways share ownership can be manipulated rather than on the relationship of the corporation to its environment. To the Shareholder, the corporation is merely money in another form and it can be directed and even liquidated to maximize the immediate yield on investment.

An example of the consequences of this point of view is that of the leveraged buyout (LBO). In the late 1980s, this form of stock manipulation became a black art practiced by the most sophisticated and sometimes unprincipled financial traders. These manipulators effectively mortgaged the futures of countless companies to achieve short-run increases in stock prices. When the dust of stock sales settled, the corporation and those Shareholders unaware of the LBO were left with monstrous debts which no amount of corporate growth could service.

In contrast, the Stakeholder views the benefits he or she receives from the corporation as the return on the assets held in stewardship. Even though these assets may be owned by the Stakeholder, they are seen in a larger context where there is a claim on their continued use by the corporation and actors in the environment. Thus, the Stakeholder is not only responsible for the immediate financial health of the corporation; he or she is also accountable for its impact on the physical and social environment as well as its potential for long-term survival. This is stewardship writ large where a balance must be struck between individual benefit and collective good.

Most of us are familiar with the concept of stewardship as it applies to the not-for-profit organization. In these organizations, there are groups of Stakeholders which direct its activities. They generally own its assets "in trust" and are charged with preservation of assets and achievement of corporate goals. It is the latter aspect of their stake which is important for the Transformal Paradigm. By concerning themselves with goals, Stakeholders are raising their corporate consciousness to a level that is appropriate in a global business environment. For these stewards, assets are a means to goal attainment and not a goal in and of themselves.

If we apply this definition of stewardship to the private corporation, we have a sense of who the true Stakeholders might be. They are those who have an interest in the goals of the organization and the social and personal benefits they represent. Their major emphasis is, accordingly, on the preservation of the organization and on the enhancement of its capacity for goal attainment. Their stakes include, as a result, not only economic investments. They also incorporate a "trust" interest in the corporation which takes the longer view as to social relevance and measures success in terms of both economic and non-economic benefits.

The concept of Stakeholder as steward, implies that the corporation is directed by many, diverse interests. These interests are held by people and organizations who do not directly control the corporation; they are those affected by its actions. These groups include those who work in the organization and those who consume its products and services. In addition, Stakeholders include all persons and agencies in the business environment whose opportunities and quality of life might be affected by the corporation.

Thus, the Stakeholders in modern corporations are almost without number and they cannot come together to take collective action. They must rely on managers to give form to their concerns and to take actions which are in keeping with them. This puts Stakeholder interests at the very core of all management activity. They force a broad view of corporate goals which includes financial, business and social objectives. This is an important aspect of the Transformal Paradigm shift which, to say it again, makes money a means and not an end.

For the traditional Shareholder, issues which do not directly affect share price and return on investment are matters of public, and not corporate, policy. As far as Shareholders are concerned, the social implications of corporate action are of little interest to them. At best, Shareholders react to the public interest and attempt to shield their activities from its scrutiny.

Why should the corporation worry about the large issues of public policy? After all, there are few single organizations whose products and services have any measurable affect on the general welfare. This is the reasoning which most clearly distinguished Shareholders from Stakeholders. It is reasoning which has led to countless corporate decisions which have measurably reduced the quality of life of both customers and the general public. It was probably best stated by Alfred Sloan, then President of General Motors, in the 1930s when he responded to DuPont's proposal to install safety glass in automobiles by saying, "It is not my responsibility to sell safety glass . . . You can say, perhaps, that I am selfish, but business is selfish. We are not a charitable institution—we are trying to make a profit for our Stockholders."

This wrong-headed view of the corporation is not dead. Between 1977 and 1982, the Beech-Nut Company engaged in systematic adulterating of its infant apple juice product. They even went so far as to transport the adulteration operation to Puerto Rico to escape regulation (Kindel, 1989). From the perspective of Beech-Nut management and Shareholders, short-run profit goals transcended the quality of life of youthful customers.

These examples make the point that Stakeholder interests are closely bound up with business ethics. There can be no adequate consideration of the whole range of modern corporate Stakeholders that does not, ultimately, center on the ethics of business actions. In other words, business decisions cannot be made from a narrow basis of profit and loss; the appropriate basis is that of quality of life of all Stakeholders.

Business leaders cannot give mere lip service to ethical principles in the Transformal Organization—they must put these principles to the test of action. And, they must be prepared to be judged in terms of the results. The power that business leaders possess is the instrument for doing ethics in business. This is the central point of the Transformal Paradigm as it related to Ownership and Control. It replaces symbols and discussion with action. It places the global issues of the nineties squarely in front of management decision makers. As Donald Jones would have it,

> In this changed business environment, the traditional ethic with its outdated assumptions is no longer able to identify and answer the major new ethical questions that the modern manager faces; ques-

tions of market power, oligopoly competition, pollution, and the quality of working life, occupational health, race relations, affirmative action, foreign bribery, consumer safety and welfare, privacy, weapons production, corporate governance, disclosure, organizational politics, conflicts of interest (1982, p. 138).

These questions require a new business ethic, one which is in tune with the interdependencies of the global business environment. This new ethic represents a true paradigm shift—from the individualistic themes of the past to a recognition of the legitimate claims of new Stakeholders. As we have noted elsewhere, "Traditional . . . approaches to business ethics focus upon individualistic themes—respect for private property, personal honesty, the honoring of contracts, employee loyalty. . . . As we close the twentieth century, significant pressure from environmental groups, consumer advocacy groups, special interest groups representing minorities and women, unions, and shareholders is making impotent the traditional, individualistic approaches to business ethics" (DeThomasis, 1986, p. 10).

This does not mean that the old ethic is dead. Instead, it is folded into a management ethic which recognizes the interests of key Stakeholder groups and the interdependencies among them.

The three Stakeholders shown in Figure 6.1 are quite familiar to managers. Business leaders have always dealt with the concerns of Investors, Consumers, and Employees. This book is no exception to these practices; we've dealt with Quality of Life and Quality of Work Life issues in

FIGURE 6.1

THE OVERLAPPING INTERESTS OF STAKEHOLDERS

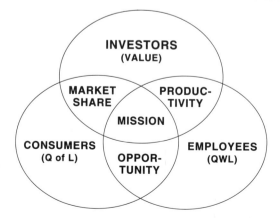

Chapter 5 and treated Value questions in Chapter 8. However, in addition to these enduring stakes, there is an interdependency which is reflected by the overlapping circles in Figure 6.1. Stakeholders no longer stand alone; they are drawn together by the complexity of business enterprise and by the interdependency imposed by globalization.

Business leaders of the nineties will need to continue to deliver on the fundamental expectations of their major Stakeholders: returning Value on Investment, contributing to the Quality of Life of Consumers, and ensuring the Quality of Worklife of Employees. In addition, and this is the paradigm change, business women and men will need to integrate concerns for Market Share, Productivity and Opportunity through corporate Mission. This is a complex balancing act which managers can perform only by attending to the unique demands raised by these interdependent interests.

Unlike the past, this balancing act puts business ethics at the center of everyday operations. As the business environment becomes more complex and Stakeholders increase in number and power, there are new trade-offs which involve redistribution of the costs and benefits of business activity. If business men and women aren't guided by ethical principles, their decisions are likely to increase the polarization of interest groups. On the other hand, if each decision is subject to close ethical scrutiny, the interests of Stakeholders can be creatively merged to increase both total benefits and the share each receives. To do this, managers must view the overlapping interests of Stakeholders shown in Figure 6.1 as *integrative* not *competitive*. In the paragraphs below, we suggest how *integration* can be pursued in the context of a global business ethic.

Managing Productivity

If there is any single variable which will define corporate success in the nineties, it is Productivity. In the traditional view, Productivity is a ratio formed of outputs to inputs:

$$PRODUCTIVITY = OUTPUTS/INPUTS$$

When this ratio is focussed on a particular Input, say, labor, and appropriate adjustments are made to cost and income measures, it is possible to examine Productivity both within the firm and across organizations. This leads to tracking of selected aspects of the ratio over time and to formation of graphs like that in Figure 6.2.

FIGURE 6.2

PRODUCTIVITY AND UNIT LABOR COST

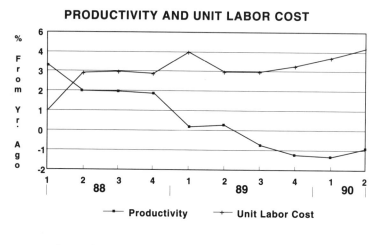

- — Productivity   —+— Unit Labor Cost

Data: U.S. Labor Dept.

If these data are taken at face value, they tell us that the unit cost of Output is rising in recent quarters. They also tell managers that either Productivity must be improved, or Labor Cost increase brought under control.

Reasoning like this leads to some very unfortunate conclusions. In recent years, managers have responded to the above trends by looking for ways to control Labor Costs. Their actions have ranged from union busting in domestic industries (Bernstein, 1990), to offshore production using cheap labor in developing countries (Peet, 1987). While these decisions might correct Productivity decline in the short run, they invariably lead to unwanted consequences in the longer view. Union busting leads to a level of labor unrest which weakens, not strengthens, Productivity. Offshore production increases Productivity but destroys markets for the outputs of the firm.

Managers are surprised and dismayed by these outcomes because they do not understand the basic dynamics of Productivity in the firm. It is but one variable in a complex causal network which must be taken as a whole in order to be effectively controlled.

Productivity is an element in a circular chain of cause and effect which dictates how Output will be attained in the organization. In this chain, ROI is used by managers to motivate workers through Wages and Benefits and as a means to increase the level of Technology in the organization. Wages and Benefits are directly linked to QWL which, in turn, defines the labor component of Productivity. As labor interacts with Technology, it makes possible greater Productivity of these investments (Nadiri and Bitros, 1980).

FIGURE 6.3

THE CAUSAL STRUCTURE OF CORPORATE PRODUCTIVITY

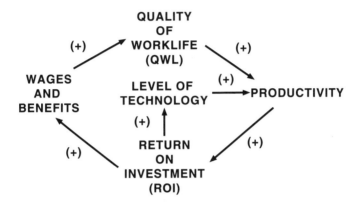

What we have here, is an expansion of the "box" at the center of Figure 5.3 to include Productivity. That is, the Social and Technical Systems of the organization interact to set a level of Productivity which determines how much Benefit can be realized. The point of this causal loop is that all links are positive (+). Any increase, however small, will be passed around the loop and, over time, multiplied to feed on itself. In a sense, there is no limit to Productivity gain, so long as research and development can uncover new Technologies.

There is, however, a darker side to Figure 6.3. Because all links in the loop are positive, any small decline in any variable will also be multiplied around the loop. For instance, a decrease in QWL due to management decisions about Wages and Benefits will lead to reduced Productivity and declines in ROI. These decrements will pressure managers to further cut Wages and Benefits and thereby set a vicious cycle in motion. This is a cycle which cannot be broken by shifting investment to Technology—for it is only in combination with Labor that Technology realizes its potential.

The upshot of all of this is that managers must pay increasing attention to the overlapping interests of Investors and Employees. This is the only way that Productivity can be improved through the "right" mix of investment in QWL and Technology.

If this isn't a persuasive argument, there is another side to the interests of these Stakeholders. They are increasingly the same people! As Drucker notes, "The reality is something that neither Jefferson nor Marx—nor indeed anyone before 1950 or 1960—could have imagined; a society of "knowledge employees" who are neither exploited nor exploiters, who individually are not capitalists but who collectively own the means of production through their pension funds, their mutual funds, their savings; who are subordinates but often also bosses themselves" (1989, p. 85).

The Investor and Employee circles in Figure 6.1 don't just touch, they are, in many organizations, identical. Paradoxically, as Drucker has said, these are the new "bosses" whose interests cannot be ignored by managers. Nevertheless, they cannot manage themselves. They, too, must dance to the rhythms of Technology and Productivity if their expectations are to be fulfilled.

Managing for Market Share

In this sector of Figure 6.1, we are viewing the investor as the controller of organization resources. Accordingly, investors determine what products and services the organization is to offer, how they are to be priced and what their level of quality is to be. It is these last two decisions that define the relationship between Consumers and Investors—they determine the Market Share that the organization can command.

Quality does not stand alone in the relationship between these Stakeholders. It is evaluated along with cost by both parties at the interface between the organization and its environment. Depending upon the cost-quality relationship, the firm can find itself in any one of four general market conditions (Strategic Planning Institute, 1985).

Each of the market conditions shown in Figure 6.4 has an effect on the vitality of the firm and its long-run competitive potential. Let's look at the implications of each condition from the perspective of the two Stakeholders involved.

Market Leaders: Every organization would like to have this relationship with its Consumers. These Leaders are highly efficient and make productive use of all inputs so that they are able to price their products at the lower end of the competitive scale. They also emphasize quality in all steps in the production process so that their goods and services set a standard for the industry.

FIGURE 6.4

COST - QUALITY
AND MARKET SHARE

On the Consumer side, these Leaders can be depended upon to deliver state-of-the-art products which will function as expected (Juran and Gryna, 1980). Moreover, they have a history of performance which builds brand loyalty. Over time, this can lead to a shared mythology in which product quality plays a lead role.

The most widely-known example of Market Leadership was that enjoyed by Volkswagen throughout the fifties and sixties. The venerable "Beetle" was endowed with supernatural qualities by its owners and its design refined to emphasize these qualities by the manufacturer. As a high quality–low cost product, it had no competition. The shared mythology of the "Beetle" was so powerful that Volkswagen found it very difficult to change the design; Consumers were, in fact, controlling the decisions of Investors.

Brand Leaders: In some ways, this is an even more desirable market condition from the perspective of the organization. It implies that products and services have such clearly superior qualities that the consumer will pay virtually any price to acquire them. If those outputs are produced efficiently, firms can be immensely profitable as Brand Leaders.

Insofar as the Consumer is concerned, it is the magnitude of the quality difference between Brand Leaders and their competitors that commands price. Often this distinction is maintained by supporting services offered by the firm and timely introduction of innovations which enhance performance. In a word, the Consumer depends upon the Brand Leader to deliver outputs which will keep the Consumer at the head of performance, technology or fashion.

The familiar example of Brand Leadership is that of IBM. Its data processing products are reliable performers and its service network is significantly better than its competition. In addition, Big Blue is continually offering new products and services which give its Consumers an edge in the information industry.

Poor but Cheap: No Investor nor Consumer wants to admit that their exchanges take place in this market. Firms don't willingly market poor, cheap outputs. When they find themselves in this market, it's usually because their products and services have fallen behind the times. They are able to turn out an out-dated product at low cost because their plant and equipment is fully amortized. And, as long as there are no competitors with new technologies or new generations of product, they can survive.

Who wants an inferior product, no matter how cheap? The answer is that many consumers will sacrifice performance to save money. Especially if their objectives are to achieve short-run savings at the expense of long-run performance. There are also those who have no alternative; the only products or services that meet their needs are the Poor But Cheap.

The example here are the countless products produced in the Soviet Union and the Eastern Bloc countries. These are notoriously low in quality and are priced in "fake" money so that their true costs of production are hidden from consumers. Since there is no choice, consumers in these nations must make do with Poor But Cheap products.

Chapter 11 Candidates: These are firms with inordinately high production costs that have not been able to realize competitive quality in their outputs. Consequently, they have a limited potential to capture Market Share and are experiencing continued loses in operation. They are, as a result, Chapter 11 Candidates whose only hope for survival is a corporate restructuring under the protection of bankruptcy law.

Often, consumers in this market segment are trapped along with the Chapter 11 firms. They have become dependent upon the firm's products and have tolerated quality declines. By continuing to patronize the firm, these consumers have enabled lax management and must share the blame for low product performance. The very existence of this market tells us that consumers do indeed "strike a deal" with companies. It also tells us that not all consumers have a clear understanding of product value and performance; many will assume that low quality products are up to industry standards.

Chapter 11 firms are most often found in industries where rapid change in technology and design are the rule. Thus, the information industry is one where Chapter 11 markets abound. How many consumers remember Osbourne computers? And how many businesses wish they hadn't bought Burroughs or UNIVAC mainframes? It's certainly true that the buyer of today must beware of purchases which are poor performers or priced inappropriately. And, it's essential to recognize that it may only be the particular product line that is bankrupt, the firm as a whole may be doing quite well.

Opportunity as a Corporate Goal

Traditionally, this has been an area of concern where corporations had to be forced into a socially-responsible position. Laws concerning Affirmative Action, employment of the handicapped and worker's rights were all enacted because the corporate conscience was unable to question opportunity-restricting practices. It is only with the increasing role of employees in the direction of corporate affairs that questions of opportunity can be raised in organizational policy debates. These are questions which have both practical and ethical dimensions and they are a key component of corporate vitality.

On the ethical side, the basic problem is one of selecting and evaluating people. Managers approach this problem with certain assumptions or premises about the criteria on which decisions are to be based and beliefs about appropriate ways to arrive at them (Stewart, 1984). These premises and beliefs are taken from prevailing societal norms about access to opportunity and what constitutes fairness in the exchange of "fair work for fair pay." In the Transformal Organization, these premises are openly stated and employees do not need to turn to external sanctions to protect their rights. Neither are managers confronted with employees who are unwilling to take appropriate direction.

The controlling premise governing Opportunity is that the corporation takes no unfair action which restricts access to the rights and benefits of participation in the organization. The key word here is unfair. Clearly, managers must select and retain employees according to their objective ability to perform on the job. They must also be able to discharge employees who are unwilling to continue to strive to meet expectations. What is unfair, is any action which bases these decisions on grounds which have no bearing on job performance.

The standard of fairness does not imply that all employees are equal or that they should be treated as if they were. Managers have a responsibility to make judgements about the contributions of employees and to reward those whose performance exceeds expectations. What makes these fair judgements is open definition of expectations, objective evaluation of performance and well-publicized scales of reward. In other words, fair Opportunity is knowing the rules and a widely-shared belief that they will be objectively applied.

This standard is very easy to see in operation. It is almost universally violated in the treatment of women by corporations in all nations. The following data from the U.S. service industries is only one instance of the continued second-class position of the working woman. So long as this sort of discrepancy persists, there is no fair Opportunity. And, from a selfish corporate perspective, there is no incentive for women to give full measure in the fairness exchange.

Unfortunately, the standard of fairness doesn't stop at the door of the Transformal Organization. There is a larger social responsibility to improve access to Opportunity through affirmative actions. Responses to this mandate take the form of seeking out those who have been denied access in the past and actively recruiting their contributions. It extends to corporate involvement in education and human development outside the firm to assist excluded groups in improving their objective qualifications.

FIGURE 6.5

COMPARATIVE WAGES IN SERVICE INDUSTRIES

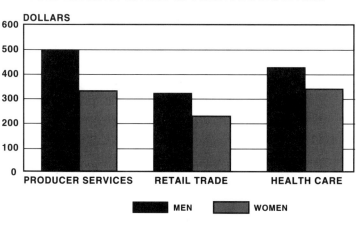

Bureau of Labor Statistics

In applying the fairness standard, the Transformal manager must always balance increased social Opportunity against the viability of the firm. Social agendas cannot be pursued to the detriment of the firm or else, at the extreme, there would be no organization and no Opportunity. A case in point is that of Control Data whose social agenda of the sixties and seventies diverted significant corporate resources from profitable activities. These policies greatly weakened the competitive position of CDC in its major computer markets and it was forced to reorganize its businesses in the 1980s (Dubashi, 1989). The result is a greatly diminished organization whose capacity to provide Opportunity is only a fraction of what it was a decade ago.

In the final analysis, the Transformal Organization is Opportunity. It is the sole best source of access to the benefits of growth and development and the only hope of many of the world's disadvantaged (Benjamin, 1988). But it cannot deliver on its potential unless managers are consistently aware of the interests of Consumers and Employees and how they can be integrated into an Opportunity structure which improves both Quality of Life and Quality of Worklife.

Managing the Corporate Mission

The "balancing acts" we've discussed above must all be integrated into a single, coherent corporate Mission. This is something that only managers can accomplish. Theirs is the responsibility to work with Stakeholders to make the necessary trade-offs so that each constituency realizes enough benefits to continue its commitment to the activities of the corporation.

The challenge to managers is captured in the word "*integrated.*" As Stakeholders see the organization, they tend to emphasize their own interests and they come to the Mission-setting exercise as if it is a competitive process in which each party gains his or her ends at the expense of everyone else. Stakeholders see Mission selection as a zero sum game where the gains of one are offset by the losses of another. Managers must take this point of view and transform it into an integrative bargain where all parties gain through their collective contributions and sacrifices of interest.

We can picture the Mission-setting problem by drawing three versions of Figure 6.1.

On the left side of Figure 6.6, we show Mission-setting as a zero sum game. The Mission is seen by all constituencies as a "pie" whose slices are to be passed around according to the relative bargaining power of

FIGURE 6.6

MISSION SETTING AND CONSTITUENCY INTERESTS

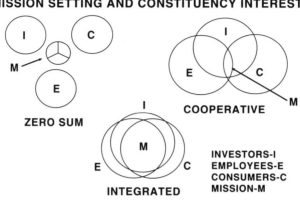

each player. If managers treat Mission-setting as conflict, there is no way to avoid confrontation and segmentation of direction in the organization.

By making Mission-setting a cooperative process where managers take the leadership in articulating the expectations of constituents, it is possible to achieve the overlapping of interests shown on the right side of Figure 6.6. To do this, managers first identify the shared concerns of those involved in Mission-setting. These are then used to find areas where there is potential agreement to increase the scope of the Mission. As the process is repeated, the "circles of concern" begin to overlap to a greater extent and the interests included in Mission take in an ever-larger share of total Stakeholder interests. This is shown at the bottom of Figure 6.6.

Throughout the Mission-setting process, managers also need to serve as the corporate conscience. They must examine the Mission from the perspective of all those who are affected by it to ensure that the organization maintains a focus on quality and that its decisions and actions conform to ethical standards. This is a matter of making the corporation accountable to all constituencies—and to the global ecology. As Johnson and Johnson states in its corporate policy:

> We are responsible to the communities in which we live and work and to the world community as well.

References

Alkhafaji, A. (1989) *A Stakeholder Approach to Corporate Governance.* New York: Quorum.

Benjamin, W. (1988) "The Ethics of Development: The Case for the Multinational Corporation," *The Hamline Review* 12 (Spring) pp. 45–58.

Bernstein, A. (1990) *Grounded: Frank Lorenzo and the Destruction of Eastern Air Lines.*

DeThomasis, L. (1989) *Monasteries on Wall Street: The Ten Commandments of Doing Ethics in Business.* Winona, MN: St. Mary's College.

DeThomasis, L. (1986) *Business Ethics and Free Enterprise.* Winona, MN: St. Mary's College.

Drucker, P. (1989) *The New Realities.* New York: Harper and Row.

Dubashi, J. (1989) "The Do-Gooder," *Financial World.* June 27, p. 70.

Etzioni, A. (1989) "Good Ethics Is Good Business," *Wall Street Journal.* February 12, p. 2.

Issues in Ethics (1988) "Thinking Ethically," *Issues in Ethics*, 1(2), 2–3.

Jones, D., ed. (1982) *Doing Ethics in Business.* Cambridge, MA: Gunn and Hain.

Juran, J. and Gryna, F. (1980) *Quality Planning and Analysis.* New York: McGraw Hill.

Kindel, S. (1989) "Bad Apple for Baby," *Financial World*, June 27, p. 48.

Nadiri, M. and Bitros, G. (1980) "Research and Development Expenditures and Labor Productivity at the Firm Level," in *New Developments in Productivity Measurement and Analysis.* J. Kendrick and B. Vaccara (eds). Chicago: University of Chicago Press, Ch. 7.

Peet, R. (1987) *International Capitalism and Industrial Restructuring.* Boston: Allen and Unwin.

Stewart, D. (1984) "Managing Competing Claims: An Ethical Framework for Human Resource Decision Making," *Public Administration Review*, January, pp. 14–22.

Strategic Planning Institute (1985) "Cost Quality Relationships in American Businesses," Cambridge, MA: Sloan School of Management.

Wallace, D. and White, J. (1988) "Building Integrity in Organizations," *New Management.* 6(1), 30–35.

CHAPTER 7

The Cybernetic Organization

ORGANIZATION DIMENSION	ALTERNATIVE PARADIGMS		
	COMMUNIST	CAPITALIST	TRANSFORMAL
MODE OF ORGANIZATION	Bureaucracy	Corporation	Cybernetic

Shifts in the socioeconomic paradigms across the globe generate a tremendous amount of uncertainty for business women and men. Demands for goods and services can take drastic new directions; competition for personnel and capital increases; and the rules of the game can be reset by new political regimes in a moment. In these times, the business organization often seems to be the only stabilizing force in a turbulent environment. It's, therefore, not surprising that business leaders focus on the structural characteristics of their organizations as they attempt to deal with an uncertain future.

Since the organization is largely under the control of managers, its internal structure can be manipulated to position it in the environments in which it does business. By giving order to the organization, business men and women are able, to a considerable degree, to shape its transactions with the outside world. If the structures they choose are well-matched to the environment, the organization is able to attain a competitive advantage which contributes to survival and profitability. When these structures are poorly fit to their environments, the organization is at risk of failure. As many organization theorists have argued, the primary task of top management is to devise structures which make the organization responsive to its environment and protective of its integrity (Lawrence and Lorsch, 1967; Miles, Snow and Pfeffer, 1976).

The relationship between the organization and its environment is one which is mediated by management according to the set of relationships shown in Figure 7.1.

On the right-hand side of this drawing, we picture a reciprocal exchange between the Organization Structure and the Organization Environment. These represent the "facts" of business life; the threats and

FIGURE 7.1

**MANAGERIAL PARADIGMS AND
THE ORGANIZATION-ENVIRONMENT RELATIONSHIP**

opportunities posed by the Environment and the capacity of the Structure to manage them. The key to the effectiveness of the Structure-Environment relationship lies in the Paradigms held by managers. These are beliefs about the Structures that "work" for given Environmental circumstances. They are conditioned by experience and formed in accord with prevailing business practices—they are what we mean when we refer to "business as usual."

When the Organization Environment becomes turbulent, many existing Organization Structures no longer work. When this happens, managers begin to receive information about both Structure and Environment (as shown by the arrows entering the Managerial Paradigms above). This information is a signal that Structural changes are in order if the organization is to preserve its competitive advantage. Whether such changes occur is dependent upon the extent to which managers have alternative Paradigms in mind along with the leadership skills to put them in place. They must shake off the dictates of conventional wisdom and turn to untried Structures in the hope that environmental turbulence can be controlled.

Fortunately, this is not a new experience for managers. Throughout the history of business activity, there have been significant changes in environmental conditions, changes which have required new structures. As new structures were tested and found to be effective, they became "ruling paradigms" which shaped the general form of business organization.

Although these structures show a pattern of evolution over time, they have a common feature. All organizations use information for the purpose of control and coordination of what they do. As Cecil Rhodes stated in the late 1800s, "Steam is my arm and the telegraph is my brain." In this metaphor, steam provides the energy for production and transportation. It is, however, useless without a "brain" which can shape its power to the ends of organization. This balance between information and process is suggested by the Traditional Paradigm of Figure 7.2.

FIGURE 7.2

**THE TRADITIONAL PARADIGM OF
ORGANIZATION STRUCTURE**

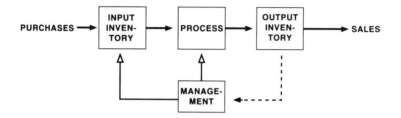

Here, the solid lines represent flows of people, resources and materials. These are acquired by the organization and collected as an Input Inventory. The Inventory is drawn upon by a Process which transforms Inputs into Outputs to be held in an Output Inventory from which Sales are made.

These three "boxes" are stocks which are the object of Management attention in a feedback control network. The dotted arrow in Figure 7.2 represents the flow of information which Management uses to coordinate the work of the organization and unshaded arrows chart the path of management control actions. Here's how this works. Management continually monitors the Output Inventory to see to it that Sales are covered and no inordinate backorder delays occur. Managers achieve this objective by directing the acquisition of Inputs and scheduling Process activities (Roberts, 1981).

This Traditional Paradigm was quite effective under historical conditions of stable demand and predictable supply. In Cecil Rhodes's day, organization processes were usually quite elementary and easily understood. Most products and services were relatively simple and input/output balances were readily discovered and controlled. Consequently, centralized control over global organizations was possible and the supporting infomation system could be designed to facilitate the objectives of organizations and empires.

Rhodes managed his far-flung activities with a complex set of telegraphic codes which told subordinates exactly what to do. However, even in those uncomplicated times, errors in communication could have catastrophic results. The student of South African history will recall the abortive Jameson raid on the Transvaal and the telegraphic errors which might have precipitated it. In fact, some suggest that the errors in Rhodes's telegraphic coding system obligated him to cover up the role of the British government in this adventure (Winks, 1969).

As organizations became more complex and geographically dispersed, control errors grew both in frequency and importance. These developments resulted in modifications to the Traditional Paradigm at two levels. First, Organization Hierarchies were created to coordinate the activities of a larger number of departments and divisions. Second, Process Control Theory was developed to smooth the functioning of ever more complicated production operations. Each of these bodies of knowledge centers on a ruling paradigm which forms the basis of much of contemporary organizational structure.

Organization Hierarchies

The metaphor underlying the Hierarchical Paradigm is that of organization as a collection of units or "building blocks." In this metaphor, each "building block" has a pre-determined role to play in the work of the organization. This is represented in a specific, stable set of exchanges with other "blocks." Thus, the Process block in Figure 7.2 receives inputs of resources and materials from the Input Inventory block and delivers its finished products to Output Inventory.

The power of the "building block" metaphor lies in its capacity to focus management attention on the exchanges between "blocks" and on summary measures of performance of each "block." This makes it possible, for example, for production managers to measure Processes by their rate of output and to adjust output by altering inputs and/or the internal arrangements of production operations. The metaphor also suggests that "blocks" can be arranged in "stacks" so that higher-level activities exert control over lower levels as we see in Figure 7.3.

In this schema, the hierarchical arrangements of "blocks" represent increasing authority so that the flow of control and coordination is generally downward from the strategic level of management through the tactical level to impact operational activities (Mesarovic, 1970: Findeisen, et.al., 1980). The same hierarchy processes an upward flow of information concerning operational performance so that decision makers can monitor the effects of their actions. We show this in Figure 7.3 in the use of unshaded arrows to represent control and coordination with dotted arrows representing the flow of information.

FIGURE 7.3

THE HIERARCHICAL PARADIGM

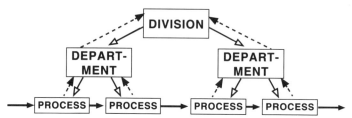

Notice, also, how this paradigm fits conventional organization structures. Several Processes are linked together at the lowest level of organization by their exchanges of resources and materials (solid arrows). These Processes are aggregated into Departments to facilitate coordination of effort at the tactical level. By bringing several Departments under a Divisional authority, the paradigm facilitates the achievement of strategic objectives across the entire organization.

What all this amounts to is that managers and employees at any given level in the organization are accustomed to direction from above. They also expect to report their performance to higher levels of authority and to be rewarded (or punished) according to their achievements. In this way, the paradigm makes for predictable behavior and for the interchangeability of personnel from one type of organization to another.

Unfortunately, the power of the hierarchical paradigm to control individual behavior is its greatest limitation. This is due to the fact that decisions of any scope cannot be made speedily by those who have the most relevant information. In a changing business environment, the responses of the hierarchical organization are limited by structure and the creativity of individual managers and employees is stifled by reporting and decision-making routines.

Process Control

Within the hierarchical organization, there are many processes which are routine and repetitive in nature. These vary from the batch processes of appliance production to the continuous processes of refineries (Woodward, 1965). These are linked sets of activities which are well-known and easily controlled using standard decision rules. For example, production managers can identify the operations needed to manufacture a toaster and they can measure the time and resources required for each step. Consequently, it is possible to apply rules about timing and coordination of activities to ensure that production goals are met.

Such rules are derived from the paradigm of Process Control where feedback of performance information is used to make management decisions. This usually involves a network of activity, information and control like that shown in Figure 7.4.

FIGURE 7.4

PROCESS CONTROL

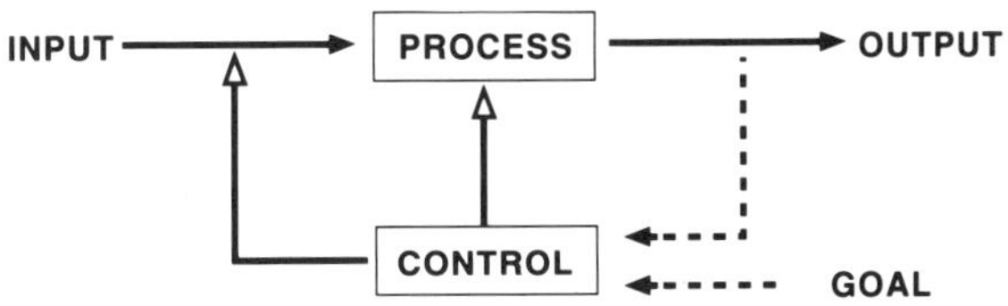

Readers will recognize that this drawing is a special version of Figure 7.1. It applies the general principle of information feedback to the specific activities of production and service units within the organization. In this paradigm, the Output of a given Process or unit is compared to a preset Goal. Depending upon the results of that comparison, changes are made in Process inputs or in the activities that make up the Process. If these changes are made correctly, Output comes into line with the Goal over time.

The behavior of Control structures of this type follows the general pattern shown in Figure 7.5 below.

In this example, the Goal to be achieved by the Process is pictured as a solid line while the actual results of the Process are represented by a dotted line. Here, we show that the Goal is changed at a point in time (A) when the process was meeting its objectives. This change results in a discrepancy between Goal and Results which is a signal to managers to initiate changes in Input or Process.

The effect of management Control is seen as a gradual increase in Output until the Goal is reached at point (B). However, due to the delays in the collection and analysis of information, managers cannot act immediately on observed discrepancies. Instead, earlier Control Inputs continue to act on the Process so that Output exceeds the Goal at point (C). This

FIGURE 7.5

THE BEHAVIOR OF PROCESS CONTROL SYSTEMS

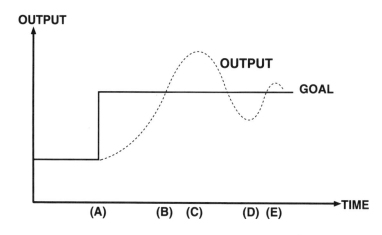

overshoot causes managers to reduce their control efforts and, due again to delays in the system, Output undershoots the Goal (D).

As time passes, these over- and undershoots are reduced in magnitude so that Output ultimately comes into line with the Goal (E). While this is almost always a cyclic process, managers can anticipate delays and minimize the amount of over- and undershoot. This is especially true for automated Process Control where the nature of the Process is well-understood and Control Inputs can be more accurately matched to the discrepancies observed between Output and Goals.

When this paradigm is applied to the organization as a whole, it provides a general strategy whereby managers can effectively control the inner workings of production and service delivery processes. By analyzing the details of these processes, managers can develop accurate mathematical models which predict the consequences of various decisions. When these models are exercised in the framework of the goals and objectives of the organization, we find that many of the problems of operational management can be programmed. This means that specific rules can be written to specify the actions needed to correct observed discrepancies between Output and Goals (Simon, 1977). In fact, many of the best-understood models have been fully programmed in that Control has been turned over to computers, as is the case in steel mills and refineries. And, the argument can be made that none of our modern production organizations could exist in its present form without the Process Control Paradigm.

Toward a Cybernetic Paradigm

But the paradigm of control theory is not limited to process management. It also extends to the larger issues of organization-environment relationships and to the strategic directions pursued by top management. This is what many writers call the Cybernetic Paradigm where the organization (and its managers) learns about "what works" by observing the effects of strategies and tactics on the organization and its surroundings.

This paradigm is based on the metaphor of the organization as a "brain" (Morgan, 1986). The organization is effectively a repository of information which is used to take reasoned, adaptive action. The components of organization and their managers process information to make decisions about activities and goals to better fit the organization to its surroundings. These modes of behavior lead to certain characteristic properties which we find in Transformal Organizations (T-Os).

T-Os	ARE MADE UP OF SEMI-AUTONOMOUS FUNCTIONAL UNITS.

The larger organization—the "brain—is a collection of smaller units—"brain cells." These are formed according to the functional requirements of the technology used by the organization. For example, a bank is the aggregate of functions needed to collect and disperse money—such as customer service, loan processing and accounting. Each unit has a set of objectives which embody its function. In banks, the customer service unit must identify customer needs, select appropriate mixes of service and deliver them efficiently. These unit objectives "add up" across the organization to enable it to pursue mission-related goals.

The organization is able to utilize the contributions of its functional components by setting their objectives. In the Cybernetic Paradigm, each unit is free to decide how it will attempt to achieve its objectives. We say that the unit is semi-autonomous in that it cannot select what its function is to be, but it can determine which activities it will use to respond to organizational expectations.

Another way to look at organization units in the Cybernetic Paradigm is to think of them as miniature organizations. Units use information feedback and process control to structure themselves and their activities. By treating the organization as "environment," they are able to make adaptive decisions which make for more productive exchanges with other units. In effect, each unit has the capacity to become an organization in itself (Wilber, 1982). We see this at work when a department or a division of an organization is "spun off" to become a completely autonomous entity. In so doing, the released unit makes use of the following principle.

T-Os	LEARN THROUGH INTERACTIONS WITH THEIR ENVIRONMENTS.

This is where the Cybernetic Paradigm differs from that of Process Control. Process Control treats goals and objectives as pre-determined reference points against which results can be measured. In the Cybernetic Paradigm, goals and objectives are also open to question. As a result, the models of organizational activity are not settled and it is generally impossible to program the decision options facing managers. There are simply too many variables involved in goal-setting and organizational change. In problems of this type, managers must turn to more general rules of analysis and to the use of insight and intuition. This is what Simon (1977) and others have called heuristic decision making where the more advanced human mental capacities are exercised.

What this amounts to, is adding another feedback loop to Figure 7.4 where information about the organization-environment interaction is used to question Output Goals. That is, when a discrepancy exists between over-all organizational Output and pre-set Goals, the question is asked, "Are these Goals appropriate at this time and in this environment?" If managers judge that Goals are out of line, they can formulate new ones and observe whether existing Processes can attain them. In this way, the organization "learns" about itself and its surroundings.

What's important about this paradigm for the nineties, is that a good deal is known about management problem solving in general and about the organization-environment relationship in many areas of economic activity. These bodies of knowledge have made it possible to create artificial intelligences which can help direct the learning activities of managers and organizations. These intelligences are computer-based representations of higher-order human thought that serve as interactive environments in which managers can test the consequences of organizational change.

The point of this argument is that the decision environment facing managers is one in which an emphasis on the systemic character of organization is the only possible way to success. By building upon the known attributes and functions of organization systems, managers cannot only control complex processes; they can reduce uncertainty in their dealings with a confusing environment. Thus, information becomes a key resource in all aspects of organization as we'll be emphasizing in Chapter 10. By concentrating on functionality and learning, organizations create the capacity to learn and to self-organize.

| T-Os | USE NETWORKS TO COORDINATE THEIR ACTIVITIES. |

The functional units which make up Transformal Organizations can be arranged in many different ways to meet the requirements of particular products/services or to best apply the core technology used to create these outputs (De, 1985). The structure selected by a given organization will depend upon the information exchanges needed to support basic processes or operations. These will necessarily deviate from the hierarchical paradigm and will take the form of networks which link functional units through information flows. Networks determine the locus of control in the Transformal Organization and provide the channels of communication whereby control reaches the proper unit or activity (Huber, 1990).

A useful example of the networked nature of Transformal Organizations is that of automated production systems. Networks resulting from the organized use of this technology are based on relationships like those shown in Figure 7.6 (McLean, et.al., 1983).

In this configuration, the basic processing entity is a workstation (WORK). Each station represents an automated process such as a numerically-controlled (NC) machine tool or robot. Workstations are connected

FIGURE 7.6

DYNAMIC NETWORK FOR PRODUCTION CONTROL

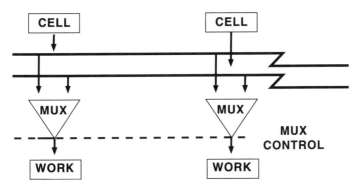

in a dynamic control network through multiplexors (MUXs) which facilitate the electronic exchange of control information. The critical feature of this structure is the controlling role played by the cell. Cells determine how the production task is to be carried out and how workstations are to be controlled. Thus, each workstation is connected to only one cell during a particular task. However, since the network is dynamic, cells can share workstations and the processing resources of the organization can be reallocated as tasks are completed.

This network is dynamic in that it can be reconfigured by the MUX Control which serves to focus workstations on organizational goals. A shop or factory, comprised of many cells, is centrally managed to make decisions as to how cells are to be assigned goal-related work. Once this decision has been made, a "select" signal is sent through the network to a particular MUX and its associated workstation is connected to a controlling cell for the duration of the task at hand. When that task is completed, the workstation is released and other cells are free to capture it as they pursue other aspects of organization mission.

In Transformal Organizations, the general principle of dynamic networking described in this example holds for all other organization units. Units or workstations which incorporate people and machines as well as those which employ only human inputs are all part of a dynamic network which changes form in keeping with changes in organization goals, technology or resources. This is the essence of our next principle.

T-Os	MODIFY THEIR STRUCTURES IN ACCORD WITH CHANGES IN GOALS AND ENVIRONMENTAL CONDITIONS.

This principle speaks to the real power of the Transformal Paradigm insofar as it influences organization structure. Because the networks described above are easily reconfigured, they enable the organization to optimize its relationship with the environment. As the organization "learns" about its capacity to manage environmental turbulence, it discovers better ways to arrange relationships among its constituent units. These insights are acted upon by making changes in control and communication networks to arrive at configurations which will make the most of organizational knowledge and resources.

Dynamic reconfigurations of organization represent a continual search for a form which will enable the organization to reduce the impact of environment on its core activities (Alexander, 1964). It involves the identification of surplus or slack resources within the organization which can be put to use toward this objective (Galbraith, 1977). It is a creative process which liberates managers from the narrow confines of bureaucracy to invent forms which are more fitted to reality. To the extent that the behavior of units and networks is known, it is possible to design alternative forms and to study their behavior through the use of simulation modelling and other design tools. This gives managers the capacity to deal with ever-more complex technologies in increasingly turbulent environments.

We need, however, to offer a caution to this mechanistic view of organization. No matter how well-conceived a given network, individual behavior and organization cultures can intervene to alter its objective potential. Consequently, managers need to be aware of the effect of populating the Transformal Organization.

| T-Os | CHANNEL HUMAN ENERGY THROUGH NETWORK-BASED ROLES. |

Managers can begin to acquire insights into organization functioning by viewing the objective network as a frame on which interpersonal relationships are founded. Objective networks provide opportunities for human interaction which, in turn, lead to the development of the whole range of social relationships; friendships, cliques, power and cultures. These opportunities enrich the dimensions of the network to affect the functioning of any of its constituent units. By addressing the human side of the network, managers can identify key social relationships and behavior influences which may affect the control the organization is able to exert over its goal-directed activity (Lincoln and Miller, 1979; O'Reilly and Roberts, 1977).

Organization networks are not, however, simply patterns of friendship and association. They express the fundamental inequality of much of organizational life; the fact that control and power are closely allied in the organization (Newman, 1979). Information available to individuals and groups and a consequence of their location in the objective network provides a basis for social power (Pettigrew, 1972). Social power, in turn, determines how organization resources are to be employed and, consequently, the ultimate input/output relationships among organization units.

By structuring the interactions among organization members, networks define the elements of a corporate culture (Deal and Kennedy, 1982). Group norms and beliefs are developed as a consequence of day-to-day interactions among employees and managers. These define the capacity of the organization to manage its affairs and its ability to deal with environmental uncertainty (Starbuck, et.al., 1978).

Thus, we see human relationships as critical elements in the design of Transformal Organizations. Social relationships growing out of network location can provide support for mission-related activity, but only if the corporate culture fosters an open attitude toward power and control. Power must be seen as merely another resource which can be dynamically reallocated without punishing those who lose control. To make this happen, managers must be continually sensitive to balancing the objective requirements for individual behavior set by the network structure with each person's needs for fulfillment and control over his or her own life in the organization. This involves the exchange of rigid hierarchies of power and control for more flexible networks which empower all members of the organization (Herbst, 1976).

Summary: Going with the Flow

Like all of our paradigm changes, the shift to a cybernetic mode of organization involves some specific re-direction of management thought. We call this "going with the flow." Managers begin to see the organization as dynamic flows of materials, people, resources and information which must be directed in order to hit a moving goal. They no longer view the maintenance of stocks of inventory, orders and assets as their primary objective.

In the process of "going with the flow" managers come to the realization that flow control is brought about by the use of information. Their task is to collect the correct information and to direct it to the point(s) in the organization where flow control decisions can be made (Roberts, 1981). As they shape information to these uses, managers "flow" the organization toward an environmentally-appropriate form.

We can see an example of "going with the flow" in the transformation of agricultural commodity trade in the U.S. in the 1970s. Prior to the explosion of world demand in that decade, trade in commodities was directed by managers who emphasized stocks. Commodities were collected in inventories where rents were charged for their storage. They were delivered to domestic users on schedules which maintained user inventories of unprocessed raw materials.

The market dynamics of the seventies changed all of this. Commodities were suddenly in continuous flow from producers to users across the globe. As a result, managers had to be able to direct these movements so that demand was met and profits were made to replace the storage income of the past. This was done by finding ways to add value to flows through improved handling and shipping practices. In that process, information became the central ingredient in a complex communication network that linked producer, shipper and user through the medium of commodity markets.

This example emphasizes the close relationship between the networked organization and its capacity to add value to the inputs it receives from the environment. From the perspective of the Transformal Paradigm, value is inseparable from organization structure and process; it is the guarantee which enables each organization unit to count on the exchanges it has with those in its network. And, it is the ultimate guarantee that the organization offers to those it touches in its environment.

References

Alexander, C. (1964) *Notes on the Synthesis of Form.* Cambridge, MA: Harvard University Press.

De, S. et.al. (1985) "Decision Support in Computer-Integrated Manufacturing," *Decision Support Systems,* 1(1), 37-55.

Deal, T. and Kennedy, A. (1982) *Corporate Cultures.* Reading, MA: Addison Wesley.

Findeisen, W. et.al., (1980) *Control and Coordination in Hierarchical Systems.* New York: J. Wiley.

Galbraith, J. (1977) *Organization Design.* Reading, MA: Addison Wesley.

Herbst, P. (1976) *Alternatives to Hierarchies.* Leiden, Holland: Nijoff.

Huber, G. (1990) "A Theory of the Effects of Advanced Information Technologies on Organization Design," in XXX (ed) *Organizations and Communication Technology.* Newbury Park, CA: Sage.

Lawrence, P. and Lorsch, J. (1967) *Organization and Environment.* Homewood, IL: Irwin.

Lincoln, J. and Miller, J. (1979) "Work and Friendship Ties in Organizations: A Comparative Analysis of Relational Networks," *Administrative Science Quarterly,* 24(2), 181–199.

McLean, C., et.al. (1983) "A Computer Architecture for Small Batch Manufacturing," *IEEE Spectrum,* 20(1), 59–64.

Mesarovic, M. et.al., (1970) *Theory of Hierarchical, Multilevel Systems.* New York: Academic Press.

Miles, R., Snow, C. and Pfeffer, J. (1978) *Organizational Strategy, Structure and Process*. New York: McGraw Hill.

Morgan, G. (1986) *Images of Organization*. Newbury Park, CA: Sage.

Newman, W. (1979) "Company Politics," *Journal of General Management*, 5, 3–11.

O'Reilly, C. and Roberts, K. (1977) "Task Group Structure, Communication and Effectiveness," *Journal of Applied Psychology*, 62, 674–681.

Pettigrew, A. (1972) "Information Control as a Power Resource," *Sociology*, 6, 187–204.

Roberts, E. (1981) *Managerial Applications of System Dynamics*. Cambridge, MA: MIT Press.

Simon, H. (1977) *The New Science of Management Decision*. Englewood Cliffs, NJ: Prentice Hall.

Starbuck, W. et.al. (1978) "Responding to Crises," *Journal of Business Administration*, 9(2) pp. 111–137.

Wilber, K. (ed) (1982) *The Holographic Paradigm and Other Paradoxes*. Boulder, CO: Shambhala.

Winks, R. (1969) *The Historian as Detective*. New York: Harper and Row.

Woodward, J. (1965) *Industrial Organization: Theory and Practice*. London: Oxford.

CHAPTER 8

The Value Added Organization

ORGANIZATION	ALTERNATIVE PARADIGMS		
DIMENSION	COMMUNIST	CAPITALIST	TRANSFORMAL
PERFORMANCE	Quotas	Profits	Value

In any business paradigm, the measure of Performance must reflect the organization's capacity to elicit the support of all constituencies and key actors. Employees and managers must not only receive compensation for their efforts, they must continue to believe in organizational mission and methods of operation. Consumers must see the organization and its products and services as a useful component of the socioeconomic system and have confidence in the ways it uses resources. And, investors must see the organization as a means to achieve their economic ends. The beliefs and commitments of all these actors turn on the Performance of organizations.

The indicators of Performance are necessarily very broad measures of organization work. They cut across all types of organization and they address the whole range of business activity. As such, these indicators permit comparisons between organizations engaged in totally different businesses. Because they are such powerful "universals," Performance indicators are deeply imbedded in their associated paradigms. They are at the center of management thinking and are supported by business practices and systems that are institutions in themselves.

Consequently, any shift in Performance indicators is resisted by beliefs, systems and behaviors which define the economic life of whole nations. This is easy to see as we consider the shift from the Communist to the Capitalist paradigms. This involves acceptance of Profit measures in place of Quotas. In communist organizations, Quotas are pervasive guides to behavior. Every operator, supervisor, and manger has his or her Quota to meet and each directs all activities under his or her control toward the achievement of the Quota. Quotas are aggregated to assess the contribution of the organization to the larger economic system. Ultimately, the Performance of the entire system is assessed by the extent to which its constituent organizations meet their Quotas.

The focus on Quotas is developed in the educational system so that it becomes part of the common language spoken by all citizens. People become accustomed to measuring their efforts against Quotas and to rewards that are directly linked to their attainment. In addition, record keeping systems and management control structures are all geared to setting Quotas and monitoring progress toward their fulfillment. In effect, Quotas are the "speedometer" of the communist system and all eyes are glued on them to assess the pace and progress of socioeconomic life.

As the Communist Paradigm gives way to a capitalist alternative, there is a wrenching change needed if Profit is to be accepted as a measure of Performance. Organizational inputs and outputs must be measured in terms of real money and they must be priced in a competitive market which reflects their potential contribution to business activity. Central planning and Quota-setting must be replaced by "votes" in the free market which may dictate the production of whole new mixes of goods and services. In the Capitalist Paradigm, Organization Performance is gauged by the capacity to generate Profits which are, in turn, used by the organization to reward its employees and investors. These are the basic institutional changes which can, to some extent, be created by legislation.

There is, however, a deeper and more essential change involved in the shift from communism to capitalism. This has to do with the beliefs of citizens, workers and managers and with their behavior in organizations. People must be educated to accept monetary measures of their activities and organizations. Changes are also needed in business practices and systems which must be totally overhauled to track Profit measures and monitor substantive rather than symbolic Performance.

A change of this magnitude—a true paradigm shift—involves the overthrow of old myths and metaphors in favor of unfamiliar alternatives. But, more to the point, it requires the replacement of the institutions, behaviors and systems which make up organizational work. As we can already see in the Communist Bloc countries, these are changes which are not easily brought about; they can lead to massive unemployment, erratic markets, loss of organizational control, and a host of unfilled expectations on the part of all economic players.

What this means for our Transformal Paradigm is that we cannot hope to make major changes in the underlying beliefs and behaviors of the capitalist system. Instead, we need to build our measures of Performance on trends already under way. In this way, the Transformal Organization can take root in the practices of capitalism and shape it to the requirements of the global ecology. The way we'll go about this is to play on the emerging importance of Value in the Capitalist Paradigm.

Value and Organizational Performance

The social and economic developments of the 1980s have already brought about significant changes in the capitalist view of organizational Performance. The long-standing focus on accounting Profits has been gradually replaced by a concern for the Value of the organization. Much of the impetus for this shift in focus came from a growing disenchantment with accounting practices and bottom-line measures of Profit. An example shows why this occurred.

How did USX (U.S. Steel) go from the biggest money loser among Fortune 500 companies in 1983 (1.2 billion dollars) to the 37th most profitable in 1984 (493 million)? Simple. By making such accounting maneuvers as: sale of assets, reducing inventories, and adoption of new accounting systems. Only 157 million dollars of the reported profits were generated by operations (Norton, 1985). Clearly, some alternative Performance measure is needed to give investors and managers a more accurate picture of the economic viability of the organization.

Value is the alternative to Profit. Value is the net economic benefit produced by the organization after all costs have been deducted. It is based on the notion that benefits cannot be generated without sacrifices and that every decision to invest or act involves giving up some alternative. Consider Benjamin Franklin's advice:

> Remember that Time is Money. He that can earn Ten Shillings a Day by his Labour, and goes abroad, or sits idle one half of that Day, tho' he spends but Sixpence during his Diversion or Idleness, ought not to rekon That the one Expence; he has really spent or rather thrown away Five Shillings besides (Franklin, 1748).

Time, effort and money can all be put to other uses. And, each use has a unique level of return or benefit. This makes it possible for us to compare alternative courses of action and to choose the venture of highest Value. From the perspective of business leaders, Value maximization becomes a primary objective and cash flow the operational measure of the value-generating capacity of the firm.

The challenge for business unit managers can be summed up in two words: managing value. To meet that challenge, every business unit manager should know the answers to such questions as: What is the cash flow-based value of our business? How does this compare with its potential market value? How much value will our current plans and strategies create versus business as usual? . . . The trick is to focus not on traditional accounting measures, but on cash flows. (Copeland, et.al., 1990, p. 23)

When business women and men go about answering these questions, and taking appropriate action, they are engaged in Value Management. This is an exercise in leadership which takes place at the interface between the Business Environment and Corporate Strategy as pictured in Figure 8.1.

Although we have reviewed many of the features of the Environment in earlier chapters, we need to be sure that it's clear how they set the stage for Value Management. Let's take a closer look at the three Environmental features identified above.

The Business Environment

The main feature of the Business Environment of the nineties is its turbulence. There are no "givens" concerning Finance, Markets or Dynam-

FIGURE 8.1

VALUE MANAGEMENT

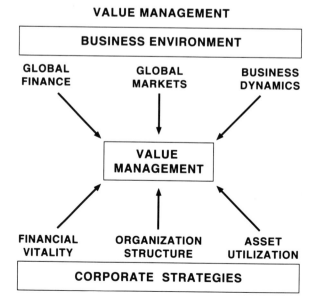

ics that can give managers a simple "handle" on the challenges facing them in the years ahead. Instead, the future calls into question nearly every standard operating procedure along with its underlying reason for being. This is what makes Value Management so important; it's a new ballgame where managers cannot rely on tried and true game plans. Here are the reasons why they can't:

1) Global Finance: When managers first began to take note of turbulence in the business environment, they observed that Capitalist economies weren't creating sufficient wealth to support needed investment. As Drucker stated in 1980, inflation, changing population structures and increased business costs all tended to suppress capital formation (Drucker, 1980, p. 28 ff). Surprisingly, these circumstances haven't destroyed capital markets, nor have they reduced the magnitude of business investment. As Copeland (et.al) notes,

> The volume of newly issued high-yield bonds . . leaped from $2.1 billion in 1980 to $27.8 billion in 1988. . . . Similarly, leveraged-buyout financing shot up from $0.8 billion in 1979 to over $50 billion in 1988—more than a fiftyfold increase in eight years. Today, market participants continue to talk of a glut of venture capital funds, and the large supply seems to be driving down interest rates (Copeland, et.al., 1990, p. 6).

Clearly, there is capital out there. It may not be new wealth, but it's an investment resource which is continually in search of high returns at acceptable levels of risk. In the developed world, it's pension funds which supply much of the investment capital. In newly industrialized countries, these monies come from the savings of workers. In a global financial market, these resources constitute an immense pool of capital in which business leaders can angle for support. Those who control these resource pools must generate maximum returns in order to provide the benefits expected by their participants and depositors.

All of this capital is increasingly liquid and able to be directed at attractive investments anywhere in the world. It's the last clause in this sentence that makes for a turbulent Capital Market. The modern investor and/or the manager of his or her funds, has access to investment opportunities across the globe via telecommunications networks that connect financial centers (Business Week, Nov. 5, 1990). The ability of the Japanese investor to move yen from Tokyo to New York to Frankfurt makes for competitive bidding on the part of borrowers.

Each must set a lure of potential return which will attract the needed funds.

In the final analysis, business leaders cannot fish in the Global Capital Market without paying attention to Value. As recent studies of capital markets have shown, investors are driven not by corporate financial statements, but by the underlying Value of the business enterprise. They are looking for future cash flows which will give them an acceptable return over and above the risks they must take. This point of view can be summarized in a simple "equation" which defines Value in terms of alternative investments.

VALUE = RETURN ON INVESTMENT - ALTERNATIVE RETURN

Each of these "returns" must be adjusted for their associated risks. Thus, the returns available on a "riskless" investment (such as government securities) forms the basis for the decisions of the investor who will move capital to investments which generate a higher return after risk discounts have been applied.

The growing importance of Value in the Global Financial Market sets the stage for the Transformal Leader. He or she must compete aggressively in the Global Financial Market by offering Value—where Value is measured by the present Value of future cash flows discounted for risk.

2) Global Markets: The cash flows we are talking about are the results of the firm's activity in a Global Market. This, too, is a turbulent environment where demand is continually refocussed by innovative producers. In addition, the rules which govern competition are changing in favor of open markets. State-owned industries are being sold in communist nations. Western countries are deregulating many of the service industries and, tariff barriers are being lowered, making—as in the European Community—entire regions where competition is fostered by free trade.

These are the basics which create the opportunity for a Global Market. The Market itself comes about as consumers share knowledge about products and services. Their common perceptions define global tastes and the level of quality they expect from producers. This is a market where loyalty is fragile, where market share rests heavily on the balance between cost and performance.

To be an effective player in the Global Market, firms need to recognize that Value goes beyond the boundaries of the organization. It is the ultimate definer of potential cash flow in that small shifts in Value can result in major gains and losses of market share. An example of the volatility of Global Markets is the change in market position experienced by Caterpillar Tractor. Cat has been a long-standing supplier of high cost-high quality construction machinery. It has also dominated the international market for heavy machinery since the 1930s. Cat's position was finally challenged in the 1970s by Komatsu which took a significant share of Cat's customer base through a Value strategy. Komatsu decided to produce a product of comparable quality at a lower delivered cost. Komatsu made these products durable enough so that they did not need to go head to head with the Cat dealer organization. The lesson is clear. No market share is safe. Any position can be effectively attacked using a Value strategy which calculates the costs of benefits of products and services from the perspective of the consumer.

The paradigm shift here is not so much that of some new type of market; it is one which fundamentally changes the view of the consumer. Business leaders must assume that consumers have nearly as much information about the market as do producers and that they have the capacity to evaluate costs and benefits on ever-finer scales. The decisions they make are moving from consuming to investing so that product performance becomes the central variable in purchasing decisions. The global consumer is, as a result, a seeker of Value.

For the Transformal Leader, this means that accurate estimates of future cash flows arise from comparisons of organization output against that of competitors. These Leaders reduce their dependency on historical data which can only tell them how current market share has been acquired. They see the outputs of their firms from the eyes of consumers and measure their Value in terms of the expectations of the ultimate user. They have the second of our "value equations" firmly in mind.

PRODUCT VALUE = USER BENEFITS - USER COSTS

In this equation, Benefits and Costs are both cash flows which occur over the life of the product or service. Like other cash flows, they are suitably discounted and evaluated at the time of the purchase decision. By paying attention to these flows, the Transformal Leader has a continued sense of the Global Market and the place of his or her firm in it.

3) Business Dynamics: The 1980s saw the emergence of several trends and innovations which have created a new set of Business Dynamics. These can be grouped under the headings of Process Innovation, Organizational Dis-Integration and Re-Configuration.

Process Innovation: In the not-so-distant past, businesses were bound to products and services by the organizational systems used to produce them. If a firm was in the electric appliance business, it stayed there and, in most cases, continued to make the same stoves, refrigerators or toasters with only minor changes in the product. This made it easy on managers. Once market share had been captured, it could easily be held by cosmetic alterations to the product line. Because the operations used in production were highly specialized, it was difficult for a competitor to enter the market. And, there was a high premium for refining the product line as there were few viable options for the firm.

During the seventies and eighties, this mode of operation was challenged and, for the most part replaced, by flexible production models (Ammentorp, 1988). These models are based on the fact that large product families have standard components which are shared by all family members. Thus, control systems are to be found in most electrical and mechanical products and most services require some sort of customer data base. These common elements can be readily re-distributed to new products/services within a family so that the organization can move into new markets quickly and efficiently. Flexible production systems have replaced antiquated production paradigms and given managers a greatly expanded set of options for generating cash flows.

Organizational Dis-Integration: There has always been a myth of dominance in the business community. Once an organization is a member of the Fortune 500, its future is assured. Like many of our favorite myths, this is almost exactly the opposite of the facts. If we look back to the top 100 companies in 1917, there are only 16 which have remained in that category in similar rankings in 1945, 67 and 68 (Newcomb, 1987, p. 162). These data lead to the conclusion that business success is never assured and that the more accurate myth is that there is always room at the top.

These facts of corporate life are even more true in the nineties. There is, for instance, little advantage to the horizontal and vertical integration of business activity. Consider, for example, the vertical integration of the telecommunications industry in the U.S. prior to 1984. The Bell System supplied all equipment, communications links, and services to the industry. When this monopoly was removed, new businesses sprang up overnight to provide more cost-effective products and services for selected market segments. It is common today for some vendors to lease lines and capacity from "The Bells" at volume discounts to re-sell them at a profit to end users. The fact is that any complex vertical system is vulnerable to an efficient competitor at some point in its line of products and services.

The same can be said of horizontal integration. When Sears attempted to build on its retailing capabilities to become a "one-stop" vendor of household products and services, it found that it could not coordinate unfamiliar activities. Sears became not only a poor competitor in financial and insurance markets, but lost its retailing edge to competitors like Target and Wall Mart.

Re-Configuration: The actual form of business organizations is also changing. The conglomerates organized at great cost in the 1970s were found to be inefficient and inflexible in the eighties. The supposed savings to be realized through central management were quickly submerged under a deluge of costs resulting from decision paralysis in dispersed operating units. What "merger maniacs" found out is that these inefficiencies cost money and any member unit must be extremely profitable if it is to pay its corporate tax and still remain a competitive generator of Value.

Because complex organizations could not manage Value, they became vulnerable to takeovers. It was possible, in the early eighties, to find large numbers of conglomerates where real Value existed among organizational units. Such conglomerates were targets of leveraged buy outs where the buyer was assured of discharging debt and making a profit. In other words, the corporation could be re-organized to become a much more efficient producer of value. This is the central concept captured in our third "value equation."

$$\text{BUSINESS VALUE} = \text{VALUE OF COMPONENTS} - \text{ORGANIZATION COST}$$

These, too, are values measured by discounted cash flows over time. Any business which cannot generate sufficient increments to Value above that produced by its components must be re-organized. This can either take place at the level of basic processes or at the corporate level. In either case, it is Value which drives Business Dynamics in the nineties.

Corporate Strategies for Value Management

There are, fortunately, a variety of effective Strategies which business leaders can employ to counter the effects of environmental turbulence. We've identified three such Strategies in Figure 8.1; in the following paragraphs, we outline each and show how it helps to reduce the impact of turbulence on the firm.

1) Financial Vitality

It should be clear from the above discussion that cash flow is everything. Business men and women have known this for centuries and, perversely, have created accounting systems and decision rules to mask the importance of cash. Their attention was focused on profit and on the momentary returns on investment. In fact, it wasn't until the publication of Accounting Practices Bulletin 19—in 1971—that these rules were even marginally reflective of the cash position of the firm. That Bulletin required the production of a "Statement of Changes in Financial Position" which was to show the sources and uses of funds in the organization. While this document does not make a clear transition of focus from profit to cash flow, it is indicative of the growing importance of cash to Financial Vitality. As Omar Khyyam would have it, "Ah, take the Cash and let the Credit go!" (Rubaiyat, XIII).

Taking our guidance from this line, it follows that all investment decisions, whether inside or outside the firm, must be based on the Value of the relevant cash flows. Value, here, refers to Present Value which means that the cash flows over the life of the investment must be discounted to present time. This involves the use of what financial managers call the Capital Assets Pricing Model (CAPM), (Rao, 1989). It is a series of steps whereby any venture or project can be systematically valued in comparison to other investment alternatives. Since the CAPM makes use of several variables which must be carefully estimated, it's easier to comprehend in flow-chart form.

FIGURE 8.2

THE VALUATION PROCESS

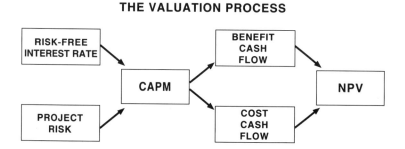

When this model is put to use, investors and/or managers must focus their attention on the following variables.

Risk-Free Interest Rate: As we've noted earlier, this is the rate of return available on government securities in the marketplace. Within the firm, the Risk-Free Rate (RFIR) is the return on investment in the firm as a whole. If we assume that the stock of the firm is correctly valued in the market, this is the return that an investor could expect from a purchase of its shares. What this means is that the marketplace has pooled the risks of all the firm's activities. Managers must, therefore, determine how the risks associated with the proposed project add to or detract from the overall risk of the firm. To do this, Project Risk needs to be estimated.

Project Risk: What we need to determine in this instance, is the systematic risk associated with the project. It is a measure of the volatility of project returns as compared to the level of returns of the firm (internal) or the market (external). It is estimated by taking into account such factors as: internal investment practices, contribution of the project to total output, susceptibility of the project to the external economy and uncertainty of output (Callahan and Mohr, 1989).

The estimation of Project Risk is probably the key issue in valuing its contribution to the firm. Both managers and investors need to take an analytic view of the organization and the "fit" of the project into its current activities (Boyadjian and Warren, 1987). If they are able to quantify the uncertainty associated with project outcomes, they can come up with an estimate of risk which can help to rationalize the investment decision.

With the RFIR and Project Risk in hand, the CAPM can be used to compute a Discount Rate for the project. This is a straightforward calculation as:

$$\text{EXPECTED RETURN} = \text{RFIR} + \text{PROJECT RISK}$$

which shows that the returns from any project must reflect the associated risks.

Cost and Benefit Cash Flows: Each quarter or year, the project will require investment to cover its Costs. At the same time, it is expected to generate Benefits in the form of cash flow. These two flows must be estimated for each time period. They, too, are uncertain and allowances must be made in the analysis to reflect errors of estimate. This can best be accomplished by the use of probability theory which effectively weights each estimate by a measure of confidence in it. The accuracy of estimates can be improved by paying attention to circumstances in the firm and the market which may alter cash flows. By linking cash flows to different scenarios, it's possible to reduce uncertainty in the valuation process.

Life Cycle: The cash flows of interest occur over a finite period of time. For the investor, this is usually the length of time he or she plans to hold the investment. For the manager, it's more complicated in that he or she must estimate how long the project will remain viable. His or her estimate must, accordingly, take account of start-up, market penetration and obsolescence if it is to contribute to an accurate assessment of project value. Projects can have infinite Life Cycles, as is the case for Classic Coke; or they can be extremely short like Pet Rocks. When making the Life Cycle choice, it's generally useful to carry out the Value analysis for several scenarios so that the implications of time-frame errors can be clearly understood.

Net Present Value: The end point of the Valuation Process is the computation of Net Present Value (NPV). This is simply the sum of the Benefits Cash Flow less the sum of the Costs Cash Flow over the Life Cycle of the project. In taking this sum, we use the Expected Return rate to discount cash flows to the present time. Net Present Value gives us a focus on Financial Vitality according to the fourth "value equation"

FINANCIAL VITALITY = NET PRESENT VALUE

where NPV is summed across all investments. Because it is calculated with reference to the market, NPV is a true measure of the extent to which management has been able to create Value. And, by basing NPV on cash flow, it's possible for managers and investors to determine how the firm has produced Value.

2) Organization Structure

The principle at the core of this strategy reads something like this. Organization adds Value to selected collections of business activity. If this weren't so, why should business leaders be committed to expanding their organizations? When a company purchases a controlling interest in another firm, it is done under the assumption that Control (organization) produces Value. Similarly, expansion of current activities into related products and services is generally initiated when managers believe that these new ventures can be organized in a manner that will add significant Value to the corporation. While these assumptions are generally true, business men and women must always put them to the test of cash-flow analysis. They must do this because organization doesn't always add Value.

There are many business concerns where components or activities are siphoning cash from the corporation. These activities generally show a profit on the corporate balance sheet. However, they don't measure up to the "return on risk" standards we've set for investment. Put another way, these low-performing activities should be moved out from under the corporate umbrella. Both they and the corporation are likely to be better off by re-organizing.

Here is the strategy. If organization adds Value to business enterprises, re-organization options should always be on the manager's desk. Then, alternative organization structures can be evaluated and a configuration chosen which will add maximum Value to the resources of the firm. If

FIGURE 8.3

FRAMEWORK FOR ANALYSIS OF CORPORATE STRUCTURE

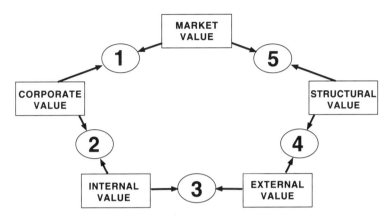

managers do not pay attention to re-organization options, their corporations will be targets for raiders. Investors will identify potential untapped sources of Value in the unmanaged organization and will move in to do the work management has neglected.

What this implies is that the Transformal Leader is, at heart, a raider of his or her own corporation! This is what Copeland and his colleagues had in mind when they proposed the restructuring framework shown in Figure 8.3. (re-drawn from Copeland, et.al., 1990, Figure 2.3)

Each of the five "boxes" in this Figure represents a valuation of the firm and its associated activities. Market Value is measured by the price of the firm's stock. Corporate Value is the return on cash flows associated with the firm's activities "as is." Internal Value represents the potential for Value generation within the organization through selected improvements in operations. External Value is essentially the "break up" price that the organization's components would bring if sold. And Structural Value is what the firm might achieve through re-organization.

These values are all calculated by analyzing current and projected cash flows and their potential return. They result in five Gaps which can be viewed as management opportunities.

Gap 1: Market Perceptions: This refers to the possibility that the firm might actually be worth more (or less) than its Value in the marketplace. When this Value Gap is large, business leaders can take measures to re-structure ownership of stock. If stock is overvalued, there is a perception of corporate strength which can be leveraged to obtain new capitalization. When the stock is undervalued, the corporation may re-purchase it to increase its controlling interest.

Gap 2: Operating Opportunity: Most organizations can improve their Value by selectively investing in their business activities. To do this, managers must continually examine each business line and stay on top of operating options. By shifting internal investments to strategic targets, managers can make significant improvements in the Value of the corporation.

Gap 3: Divestment/Acquisition: There are, on the other hand, times when the Value of certain activities is greater in the marketplace. When this occurs, managers must evaluate the potential return on divestment as compared with returns on continued operation. This comparison is not limited to the current activities of the firm. Managers should be continually sensitive to businesses which are undervalued by the market. These are acquisition targets which can be brought into the corporation to improve its over-all valuation.

Gap 4: Corporate Structure: This is a sort of "maximum strategy" Gap. It raises the question, "Can the firm be re-organized to add significant value to its activities?" After all of the above three Gaps have been addressed, there may be re-organization steps that managers can take to move toward a configuration which adds maximum Value to corporate resources.

Gap 5: Raiding: This is the ultimate test of business leadership. It takes us back to the proposition that the Transformal Leader is an "in-house" raider. What this really means is that managers make the same calculations as external raiders and that they act on their analyses. When a firm comes "in play," it is an indication that management hasn't exercised stewardship over corporate resources. If "raided" managers benefit from a takeover, they have turned their ethical responsibilities to investors and employees into private gain.

As these Gaps indicate, Organization Structure is not a single strategy. It is a set of decision options where the Value of the corporation is analyzed under different organizational configurations. Structural decisions are based on strategies which keep the fifth "value equation" at the forefront of management thinking.

VALUE ADDED = CORPORATE VALUE - VALUE IN MARKET

3) Asset Utilization

The above strategies build a solid Value base for the corporation. Managers who follow the practices outlined above have a useful "handle" on the tangible assets of the firm. They cannot, however, limit their attention to those elements of the organization that are easily measured in the market. To be effective in the nineties, business leaders will need to take the intangibles into their calculations of Value. If they fail to do so, they will be unable to benefit from the contributions of their knowledge workers and the commitments of consumers and employees.

Using intangible assets in a total asset utilization strategy means that the value generation capacity of each asset must be included in an assessment of corporate Value. This "total" strategy takes account of the whole spectrum of corporate assets as well as the interactions among them (Itami, 1987). In Figure 8.4, we show an array of assets which includes both tangible and intangible elements of the corporation.

FIGURE 8.4

THE ASSET VALUATION NETWORK

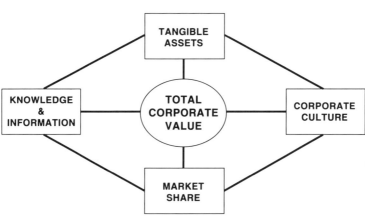

We already have a good idea of how Tangible Assets are treated in the Transformal Paradigm. What about the other asset pools in Figure 8.4?

Market Share: This is the most "tangible" of the intangibles. It is measured by the brand identification and goodwill the corporation has accumulated in the marketplace. It is sufficiently tangible to be included in accounting practices where it makes up an important part of corporate valuation (Holgate, 1988). Goodwill is also widely recognized by managers and investors; so that it is often a major consideration in restructuring decisions.

Like other valuables, Market Share is transitory. It can be managed to either gain or lose in Value. It can serve as an umbrella under which new ventures can prosper—as is the case with Walt Disney enterprises. Market Share can, paradoxically, lose its value to the firm if it becomes generic in the marketplace (Xerox) (Hall, 1989). Whatever its value over time, there is little argument with the proposition that Market Share adds Value to the firm.

Market Share also delivers Value through the interaction of the firm and its customers. These exchanges permit two-way flows of information which help the corporation track market needs as well as aiding the consumer in understanding what the organization has to offer. This can extend, as it has in many Japanese firms, to the joint design and production of both inputs and outputs. It has also drawn the consumer into service firms like banks to participate in the service delivery process. Information flows like these bond the firm and its market into a Value-producing network.

Knowledge and Information: It's also possible to set market values on many of the Knowledge and Information assets of the firm. Some of the assets which can be priced in the market are (Smith, 1988, p. 147):

    a: workforce
    b: advertising program
    c: computer software
    d: customer lists
    e: designs
    f: distributor and dealer networks
    g: going concern elements
    h: government approvals and licenses
    i: research and development
    j: training materials

In the valuation process, each of these assets can be assigned a replacement cost which can be adjusted for any price trends in the market. Thus, the workforce employed by the firm can be subdivided into professional or skill groups and current market values assigned.

This approach is all well and good, but it doesn't address the Value-generation capacity of these assets. Consider, for example, computer software created by the firm to manage its production operation. Such software is likely to be highly proprietary and created at substantial cost to the corporation. Is the cost of its production a good measure of its value? Hardly. Its real value is the increment of accuracy and efficiency it adds to production. This is appropriately measured by the addition to value generation in production. The software must also be depreciated as the operations it controls become obsolete. If it, and its associated production operation, are not updated, its future Value will be reduced.

The point of this example is that Knowledge and Information are integral to corporate Value generation. Thus, if managers are to realize maximum benefit from their utilization, they must determine how each asset contributes to cash flow. They must also, in the longer run, take care to allow for the depreciation of Knowledge and Information, both in estimating their Value and in providing for their renewal.

Corporate Culture: Here is our least tangible asset. The way the firm does business, how it interacts with the market and how it treats employees gives it relative competitive advantages which either enhance or detract from its Value-generating capacity. When a corporation is committed to deliver a quality product to the customer, it has the potential to gain market share. If the organization supports its employees and gives them opportunity for self-fulfillment, it can draw on a fund of commitment which enables it to realize increased cash flows from its wage and salary investments. Culture is a source of energy which can have a multiplying effect on the returns derived from more tangible assets.

Can Culture be managed in an over-all Value management strategy? The answer is a qualified "yes." It's qualified by the requirement that Culture can be managed best by Transformal Leaders. They are uniquely suited to reading the Corporate Culture and only they have the requisite skills to shape Culture toward its maximum contribution to Value. As we turn to the discussion of these leadership skills in Chapter 10, we'll try to show how Transformal Leaders energize the organizational dynamics which make up our final "value equation."

TOTAL CORPORATE = TANGIBLE ASSET + INTANGIBLE ASSET
    VALUE   VALUE   VALUE

Once again, these are values which are themselves dynamic and measured in the cash flows of the organization. They clearly state that leadership is shaping and directing flows—of cash, information, materials and human potential.

References

Boyadjian, J. and Warren, J. (1987) *Risks: Reading Corporate Signals.* New York: J. Wiley.

"The Future of Wall Street," (1990) *Business Week*, Nov. 5, 119–130.

Butler, J. and Schachter, B. (1989) "The Investment Decision: Estimation Risk and Risk Adjusted Discount Rates," *Financial Management* 18(4), pp. 13–22.

Callahan, C. and Mohr, R. (1989) "The Determinants of Systematic Risk," *The Financial Review*, 24(2), pp. 157–181.

Copeland, T., et.al. (1990) *Valuation: Measuring and Managing the Value of Companies*. New York: J. Wiley.

Drucker, P. (1980) *Managing in Turbulent Times*. New York: Harper and Row.

Franklin, B. (1748) "Advice to a Young Tradesman," *Papers*, Vol. III, pp. 306–308. Philadelphia, PA.

Hall, R. "The Management of Intellectual Assets," *Journal of General Management*, 15(1), pp. 53–68.

Holgate, P. (1988) *The Accounting Rules on Intangibles and Goodwill*. London: Deloitte Haskins and Sells.

Itami, H. and Roehl, T. (1987) *Mobilizing Invisible Assets*. Cambridge, MA: Harvard.

Newcomb, P. (1987) "No One Is Safe," *Forbes*, July 13, pp. 121–172.

Rao, R. (1989) *Fundamentals of Financial Management*. New York: Macmillan.

Rappaport, A. (1987) *Creating Shareholder Value*. New York: Free Press.

Reimann, B. (1987) *Managing for Value*. Oxford, OH: The Planning Forum.

Smith, G. (1988) *Corporate Valuation*. New York: J. Wiley.

Walter, J. (1990) *Financial Strategies for Managers*. New York: J. Wiley.

CHAPTER 9

Transforming Managers into Leaders

ORGANIZATION	ALTERNATIVE PARADIGMS		
DIMENSION	COMMUNIST	CAPITALIST	TRANSFORMAL
DIRECTION	Administration	Management	Leadership

The shelves of the management section of any bookstore show that there are two themes of surpassing interest to readers. There is a class of books which tell how to "make it" by investing cleverly or by engaging in certain kinds of business practices. The second class of works has to do with how to run organizations; how to manage, direct, control and, yes, even lead others. In these books we find summaries of experience of persons who have been successful investors and/or leaders.

Popular business books take a common form which could be loosely thought of as "religious" in nature. They contain a few general principles which, though unproven, are sufficiently grounded in common sense to give them the appearance of revealed truth. Readers are told that following these principles will result in consequences that are barely short of miraculous. There is, in most of these works, a cult of believers who follow the direction of the author-guru and come to believe in the approaches he or she advocates despite any objective evidence to the contrary.

Unfit to Manage

The titles found on a typical management bookshelf tell us a lot about what's wrong with modern management literature. It's easy, for example, to imagine that anybody foolish enough to *Swim with the Sharks* is taking a one-way trip into the jaws of disaster. Similarly, the business man or woman who tries to use the *Leadership Secrets of Genghis Kahn* will have an organization about as useful as a Mongol horde—if he or she isn't too busy defending the lawsuits that are likely to occur if such inhuman practices are used today. And, these ideas can only penetrate the mind of the *One Minute Manager* because no reader could possibly stand more than a minute of this sort of content.

What is abundantly clear from any serious study of modern management literature is that there is superficial quality to it. Titles and content appeal to managers looking for a "quick fix" for some very difficult problems. The business men and women who frequent these bookstores are living proof that they are, in Lieberman's words, *Unfit to Manage.* (1988) They are believers in a management mythology based on some simple falsehoods; a view of the world which is not only wrong, it is without substance. For none of our contemporary writers, and few of their readers, has taken the trouble to build an approach to management on the facts of global business life.

Thus, the first task in transforming managers into leaders is to identify the prevailing mythology which blocks management thought. Only then, will we be able to specify the knowledge and skills needed to make today's manager into tomorrow's leader. We've already talked about the foundations of these myths in Chapter 1 and it's easy to see how they shape management thinking toward superficial solutions. Let's look more closely at a few examples.

Myth No. 1: Labor is the problem, not the solution.

This is a management belief of long standing which, stated another way, blames workers for all business problems. When productivity goes down, workers are lazy; when poor quality products are produced, it's workers who make them; when products are too expensive for international trade, it's wages that run up their cost. Despite management agreement on these points, they are almost exactly the opposite of what's going on with American labor.

The myth of low productivity is especially important as it drives many business decisions. As we've shown in our earlier models (see esp. Figure 6.3), productivity is driven by the quality of worklife in the organization. In large part, this is the resultant of management practices and policies. Thus, if workers fail to be productive, it is management that must take the responsibility.

The same can be said for low quality products. They are usually the result of management production and cost-cutting targets. When quality control efforts are made, they are often belated and too far removed from production processes. The evidence is clear, when workers have the responsibility and authority to address quality problems, they improve quality. When management takes exclusive ownership of quality control, both defects and costs increase.

Are American workers paid too much? Only if they are forced to compete with Third World workers who have no alternative but to sell their labor at whatever price is offered. Remember, this creates the paradox of cheaper products that nobody can buy; labor without income means products without markets. Managers who go hunting for cheap labor have a total misunderstanding of this underlying relationship. The only time cheap labor works is when it is taken to the immediate bottom line of the corporate balance sheet. Any longer-run calculation of the capacity of the organization to generate Value will show that cheap labor doesn't pay—it costs.

Myth No. 2: If you can count beans, you can manage.

This myth characterizes the orientation of most upper-level managers. They are, first and foremost, managers of money. This is a point of view which sees the organization as an instrument for generating money. Thus, it is the dynamics of money which preoccupy managers, rather than issues of product performance and the quality of life of employees.

During the 1980s the emphasis on the "beans" of business created a new, world-wide, financial system where money can move electronically to the location where it can obtain the greatest immediate return. For the first time, money acquired "velocity" in the 1980s, ". . . zapping around the world for plants, parts, markets, ideas, staying where things look good, leaving fast where things look dicey" (Forbes, 5-5-86, p. 6). Taking the bean-counter metaphor a bit further, managers began to believe that they could collect more beans in their jars without growing them. They were, in effect, looking for return without concerning themselves with the quality products and services that must support business activity (Melman, 1983).

Myth No. 3: It's not what you know, it's who you know.

There has been a politicization of American business which has chiseled this myth into the structure of every major corporation. Management power and perquisites have gone largely to those who have been able to position themselves in the political structure of the organization.

According to Mintzberg,

> What characterizes the organization dominated by politics is a lack of any of the forms of order found in conventional organizations. In other words, the organization is best described in terms of power not structure, and that power is exercised in ways not legitimate in conventional organizations. Thus, there is no preferred method of coordination, no single dominant part of the organization, no clear type

of decentralization. Everything depends upon the fluidity of informal power, marshaled to win individual issues." (1989, p. 241)

In other words, the politicized organization is one which pursues individual objectives rather than corporate mission. Its responses cannot be predicted by business circumstances and it often appears to go off in unproductive directions. As political self-interest is carried to extremes, it results in the kind of "back room" trading which has dismembered more than one corporation.

The discounting of "what you know" is an integral part of this myth. Technical expertise and paradigm-related knowledge receives little attention in the politicized organization. Persons who hold the keys to the organization knowledge base are generally underpaid and seen by managers as unimportant luxuries which detract from the spoils which might be otherwise divided among those "who you know."

Since this myth plays into a general contempt for intellectualism held by many Americans, it finds little opposition in the value system of our culture (Hofstadter, 1969). All business needs of knowledge are the rudimentary principles of production. Once set in motion, these principles continue to run forever, churning out profit with only limited management guidance. Consequently, there is no concern for the intellectual capital of the organization; it is to be taken for granted.

In the past two decades, this contempt for the knowledge base of business has greatly reduced the lead of American business among its global competitors. Not only has intellectual capital been depleted in value, it has been sold to foreign competitors. "From 1950 to 1980, Japanese companies entered into more than 30,000 licensing and other technology-importing agreements for which the Japanese paid an estimated $10 billion." This is knowledge which was the foundation ". . . for virtually all the known commercial technology of the West" (New York Times Magazine, 7/8/84, p. 21). Here is concrete evidence of the minimal importance managers assign to "what you know."

What these myths add up to is a flawed paradigm. It is a paradigm wherein business is conducted for the benefit of a limited number of owners and managers. It is business measured by a few financial indicators which take no account of long-term corporate and social value. Finally, it is business which is an irrational power game where the future is bargained for personal gain.

The most serious consequence of this paradigm lies in its impact on management. There are now generations of managers who are adept at the political processes of organizational life; people who guide their behavior by self-interest. More importantly, these managers are those who demean the contributions of labor and ignore the knowledge base on which business is constructed. They are trained in our business schools in rituals which are as obsolete as those of the Ghost Dance. And, their beliefs are about as functional as those held by the warrior followers of Wvoka.

The Transformation of Managers

The central point of this chapter is that managers must be transformed into leaders if the transformal organization is to be effective. We realize that there's a lot of transforming going on in this sentence; both organization and administration are in flux. However, these are changes which are essential to match the organization to its environment and to give business leaders the capacity to see and seize opportunity.

Bennis makes the point that "Leaders are people who do the right thing. Managers are people who do things right" (1989, p. 18). This is a classic dichotomy which has plagued organizations for at least the last 100 years. Leaders are expected to have an almost mystical vision of corporate futures while managers slog through the mud of daily operations. While there may have been some truth in this division of labor in the past, the organization of the nineties cannot separate its fundamental activities from the threats and opportunities offered by its environment. Leadership and management must come together and all managers must undergo a transformation which will make them more leader-like.

Like all of the other changes we have proposed, this too is a paradigm shift. It involves overthrow of the mythology which has supported management to date and acceptance of new myths, metaphors and models which bring management and leadership closer together.

The shift to a leader paradigm can be set in motion by considering several myths which offer useful alternative perspectives to those described above.

Transformed Myth No. 1: People power the organization of the nineties.

This turns old Myth No. 1 on its head. People aren't the problem, they are the solution. This, however, is not an easy myth to embrace in the current climate of management opinion. In fact, the "fix" for any organization problem of today is to blame employees, reduce staff and factor people out of the solution. From this point of view, people are just one of many resources; easily replaceable and not especially important to the work of the organization.

In order to accept this Transformed Myth, leaders must understand that people represent the knowledge and energy needed to propel the organization into the future. Consequently, they are the last resource to be reduced and the first to be included in the process of identifying new ventures. They carry the knowledge which gives the corporation its competitive advantage. Theirs is the commitment which promotes corporate identity and provides the vitality needed to respond to the challenges of the business environment.

Leaders can apply this Myth by finding ways to unleash the creative energy of employees. This is what Stewart calls "Team Entrepreneurship"; the interdependence of the corporation and its people (1989). This concept implies that it is the team of employees and managers which sets corporate goals and the team which determines how resources are to be allocated to attain them. This is in sharp contrast to the notion of employee as expendable resource. Instead, employees are the organization and no future value can be generated without their involvement.

Interdependence also changes the relationship between labor and management from adversarial to collaborative. While unions may continue to exist in the transformal organization, they become more interested in increasing the size of the pie than in getting larger pieces of a smaller dessert.

There is another side to this Myth which leaders cannot ignore. Employees are, increasingly, the owners of corporations through their pension funds. As a result, there is a compelling reason to involve them in the governance of the organization—they have the power to set its direction "in the large." What managers haven't accepted is the need to involve employees in setting directions "in the small." Instead, they have engaged in union bashing to further polarize organizations in management and labor camps that talk to each other only in formal adversarial bargaining—if at all.

In a larger sense, the Myth makes a case for co-determination of corporate direction by management and labor. This is a well-established practice in several European countries—in fact, it is a legislated mandate in what was West Germany (Kuhne, 1980). Co-determination is a means whereby the corporation can access the knowledge and commitment of employees as well as their considerable financial resources. When it is denied, the organization becomes an empty shell which may be profitably shifted across the financial playing field so long as it is never examined as to what's inside.

Transformed Myth No. 2: If you don't save your seed corn, there will be no crop next year.

This Myth continues the horticultural opposite of the notion that "If you can count beans, you can manage." But we didn't choose it for that reason alone. There is, in the mind of the bean counter, an emphasis on the present which is reinforced by financial practices and documents. It is an emphasis which leads to the "eating of seed corn" to make the bottom line look good without concern for whether there will be a bottom line in the future.

The Transformal Leader is, in this Myth, the good gardener who saves enough seed for an expanded crop next year. He or she is the developer who uses that seed to improve the size and quality of the corporate crop. To do so, the Leader needs to see his or her "seed" as a mix of knowledge and people which can be made to thrive in the "garden" of international markets.

Creating a sturdy seed stock is a matter of constantly evaluating and pruning the knowledge base of the corporation. Transformal leaders are, in a sense, "paradigmers" who have a broad understanding of the knowledge structures which give the organization its competitive edge. They are sensitive to the dynamics of paradigm change in fields of importance to the corporation. By monitoring paradigm shifts, they can grow the corporate seed stock so that it produces new varieties of products and services which will attract customers to the corporation's stall in the marketplace.

Leaders recognize that the seeds of the corporation are in the minds of its members. Thus, there can be no development of seed without development of people. And, there can be no seed for the future if the human side of organization is weakened by the rot of poor management. People cannot be counted as beans; they are the embodiment of creative energy for the next planting season.

Transformed Myth No. 3: It's what you are that counts.

Unlike management, leadership isn't just a collection of skills to be applied to corporate problems. Leadership is an identity which is built on a sound foundation of values and supported by actions which will stand the test of stakeholder scrutiny. It is the unconditional identification of the leader with the corporation and its members; it is what Anne Dillard has called the "extravagant gift" (1974).

Giving the extravagant gift involves giving up many of the symbols and advantages associated with contemporary management. There can be no more bonuses paid to those who managed the decline of organizations. Nor is there a place for the conspicuous consumption of corporate resources by those in charge. In place of these actions, we can expect to find the transformal leader giving of him or herself to more closely identify his or her future with that of the organization. They are the organization—and that's what counts.

The Corporate Village: A Metaphor for Leaders

Throughout this book, we've suggested many metaphors to help readers gain an understanding of the transformal organization. Most of our metaphors have focused on economic systems at the national level or on the corporation as a whole. They provide a background against which leaders can paint their vision of the human side of organization. While each leader will have his or her own favorite metaphor to describe corporate life, we can draw an image from the above myths which offers a powerful alternative to the metaphors currently in vogue among managers.

The transformal metaphor resulting from our debunking of ancient management myths is one where people and their contributions define the future of the corporation. We call this the Metaphor of the Corporate Village. We have chosen this title to suggest that there is much to be learned from the social and economic life of the village. Especially when these lessons are considered in the context of the set of global forces which define modern business.

The central feature of the Corporate Village is that its effect is not limited to a narrowly-defined set of economic values. It is a social entity where employees, customers and stakeholders obtain both value and values to give direction and meaning to their lives. Thus, the transactions each person has with the corporation are measured on several scales; value, opportunity and commitment. The Corporate Village metaphor helps leaders weave these strands into a coherent social fabric which gives the organization the vitality it must have in order to cope with the environmental dynamics of the nineties.

Value: In Chapter 8 we made the case for value in economic terms. While this must remain the primary concern of transformal leaders, it is not the sole contribution of the corporation. Business organizations help customers and employees define other important aspects of economic and social life. These are values which indicate how individuals and groups of people are to be treated in business transactions and how their wants are to be met by the products and services of the corporation. This is the social side of the Corporate Village.

Like other villages, the Corporate Village recognizes that "we are all in it together." Every action of the corporation has an effect on the life of the village in both present and future time. If the corporation is a polluter, it will have to live in its own mess; if it helps strengthen the social fabric of its village, it will be praised in the present and supported in the future; if it grows and prospers, it will help the village survive new challenges.

In the Corporate Village, the transformal leader is one who builds a consensus among employees and stakeholders as to what the corporation stands for. The leader of the Village is very much like the head of more primitive villages. He or she has the welfare of all members of the Village in mind at all times and sees every business decision in both economic and social terms. Village leadership is, however, more than a calculation of economic and social outcomes. It is a sense of development of corporate futures which goes hand in hand with the dollars and cents of business dealings.

Fortunately, there are modern versions of the Corporate Village which enable us to see these values in action. In their study of the Basque cooperative, Mondragon, the Whytes have found an instance where social and economic values are at the center of all business activity. As they see it,

> In Mondragon, the generation of profits or surplus is a limiting condition but not the primary driving force. The distinction is between means and ends. Leaders of Mondragon recognize profits as the essential means for achieving their ends of social and economic development (Whyte and Whyte, 1988, p. 199).

Leaders of the Corporate Village are instruments whereby all stakeholders can define the values important to them. They also have the responsibility to see to it that these values are achieved and that the organization has the vitality to continue to pursue them into the foreseeable future.

Opportunity: The above sentence captures the essence of opportunity —open options to people to attain their personal and collective values now and in the future. And, it's mutual. The Corporate Village gains in opportunity to the extent that all of its members expand their options. It's this mutuality of opportunity that the transformal leader can direct and enhance.

Leaders make opportunities for all employees and stakeholders. They do this by knowing what the members of the Village want and what they are able to accomplish. Leaders help all members of the Village define what is possible and direct their efforts to make the possible a reality. This leads to a set of "Village-Oriented Employment Relations" much like the "Organization-oriented" pattern identified by Whittaker in his study of British and Japanese organization (1990, pp. 6-9). These are shown in Table 9.1 under Whittaker's headings of Employment, Payment, and Industrial Relations.

TABLE 9.1
VILLAGE-ORIENTED
OPPORTUNITY STRUCTURE

EMPLOYMENT:
* Those who work in the organization
  are members not workers.
* Members are a part of the organization
  for the long term and many can achieve
  career objectives without leaving.
PAYMENT:
* Pay is organization-driven and not
  market-driven.
* Pay is based on contribution to the
  organization rather than on political
  considerations.
INDUSTRIAL RELATIONS:
* Collaborative rather than adversarial.
* All members involved in decisions.

It is obvious that this Opportunity Structure is quite different from that of most Western organizations. It is one where leaders gain their legitimacy and support from stakeholders—in contrast to the power of the traditional manager which has an economic foundation. These organizations are truly Villages where leadership is based on consensus of purpose and consent of the membership.

Commitment: This attribute of the Corporate Village "adds up" the effects of values and opportunity. To the extent that leaders and stakeholders create an organization that assists everyone in attaining common goals, there is a mutual commitment between individual and organization. Both "sign on" to an agreement that each will support the other and that they will work together to resolve differences and to correct the inevitable differences that will occur.

On the side of the corporation, we find commitment to the individual member over the long run. It takes tangible form in the measure of job security offered by the corporation. It means that members are viewed as the productive capital base of the organization which is to be preserved and nurtured as priority number one. In times of economic recession, members are not laid off; instead, they are brought into discussions as to how the corporation can withstand market turbulence. In times of prosperity, members are not the last to realize benefits; they are the ones who help decide how benefits are to be used and/or distributed. In every dimension of organization life, members are involved in decisions and participants in sharing in both success and failure.

Commitment also works the other way. All members of the Corporate Village see their futures bound up with that of the organization. They are committed to its survival and prosperity. This implies that each member defines his or her own career in terms of jobs and responsibilities within the corporation. This, of course, runs counter to the external orientation of most organization professionals who see their futures in terms of specialties which can be applied in any organization. The future is a set of possibilities to which each person can give freely of the extravagant gift of his or her commitment.

A Transformed Leader in a Transformed Organization

The transformation of managers into leaders cannot be brought about by the reading of a few pages. It is a fundamental paradigm shift which changes all aspects of business administration. On the surface, the change to leadership may seem to be merely a matter of paying closer attention to people in the organization. This is what most of the modern management literature is saying.

But, the transformation runs much deeper. It requires a revision of the most cherished management myths and, more importantly, a commitment on the part of the transformal leader to a set of values which are quite different than those which have driven Western business in the past. These are values which create a bond between employees and the corporation, a bond which endures for most of the working life of the employee. In a sense, the corporation exists only to give form to the contributions of its member.

How does this transformation play in the financial circles of today? Isn't it dangerous for managers to change their values and behaviors? These are questions which any sensible manager must ask before embracing the paradigm of transformal leadership. They are difficult questions and the answers point to the risks that must be weighed by any aspiring leader.

With regard to financial risks; we believe that the clear direction of the marketplace is toward an emphasis on long-term Value rather than on short-term profits. As we've noted in Chapter 8, there has been a paradigm shift in financial management in the 1980s which supports a Value emphasis. If the corporation can mobilize its knowledge and people to focus on the generation of Value, its position in the marketplace will be strengthened.

Acceptance of transformal leadership at the personal level exposes managers to much greater risk. In this paradigm, they can no longer hide behind the symbols of power; they must engage in open exchanges with all members of the organization and exercise their leadership by argument and inspiration. These are skills which, unfortunately, are rarely found among managers and only occasionally emphasized in their training. Consequently, leaders must acquire them through a process of self - development in which they build a new identity which sees the self in the mirror of corporate social life.

The identity we are proposing for the transformal leader is one which puts people at the center of economic life and focuses energy on the achievement of social justice. It lays the responsibility for justice on both leaders and the corporation. As the U.S. Catholic Bishops stated in their 1986 Pastoral Letter,

> Every Perspective on economic life that is human, moral and Christian must be shaped by three questions: What does the economy do for people? What does it do to people? And how do people participate in it?

By keeping these questions at the forefront of corporate planning and decision making, the transformal leader is giving his or her organization a sense of purpose that will serve it well in turbulent times.

References

Agor, W. (1989) *Intuition in Organizations*. Newbury Park, CA: Sage.
Bennis W. (1989) *Why Leaders Can't Lead*. San Francisco: Jossey Bass.
Dillard, A. (1974) *Pilgrim at Tinker Creek*. New York: Harper.
Grinyer, P., et.al. (1988) *Sharpbenders: The Secrets of Unleashing Corporate Potential*. Oxford, UK: Basil Blackwell.

Hofstadter, R. (1969) *Anti-intellectualism in American Life*. New York: Knopf.

Kuhne, R. (1980) *Co-determination in Business*. New York: Praeger.

Lieberman, E. (1988) *Unfit to Manage*. New York: McGraw Hill.

McGregor, D. (1966) *Leadership and Motivation*. Cambridge, MA: MIT Press.

Melman, S. (1983) *Profits Without Production*. New York: Knopf.

Mintzberg, H. (1989) *Mintzberg on Management*. New York: Free Press.

Pinchot, G. (1985) *Intrapreneuring*. New York: Harper and Row.

Stewart, A. (1989) *Team Entrepreneurship*. Newbury Park, CA: Sage.

Whittaker, D. (1990) *Managing Innovation*. Cambridge, UK: Cambridge University Press.

Whyte, W. and Whyte, K. (1988) *Making Mondragon*. Ithaca, NY: ILR Press.

CHAPTER 10

The Information Asset: Tactical and Strategic Applications

ORGANIZATION	ALTERNATIVE PARADIGMS		
DIMENSION	COMMUNIST	CAPITALIST	TRANSFORMAL
PRIMARY RESOURCE	Labor	Technology & Capital	Knowledge

Of all the Organization Dimensions, that of Resources gives the most tangible evidence of the pressure on existing paradigms. The age-old conflict between emphases on Labor vs Capital has been raised to a new plane by the explosive growth of Knowledge. Organizations basing their approach to production and service on Labor alone are binding themselves into a pattern of cost acceleration which cannot fail to put them on the competitive sidelines. On the other hand, corporations which base their operations on Capital investments will surely be left behind as current investments and technologies are rendered obsolete by new Knowledge.

As business leaders attempt to embrace the Knowledge Resource, they will need to change their view of the use of information in organizations. In the past, information was a necessary part of control and an ingredient in strategic thinking. In the future, information will increasingly become Knowledge as it contains not only the guides for corporate action, but the opportunities for competitive use of information. A simple—if not bucolic—example shows how this paradigm shift changes corporate practice.

Land O Lakes, a major international supplier of agricultural products and services, prepares and markets animal feeds as one of its major enterprises. In the past, feeds were viewed as a mixture of ingredients and LOL made its profits by controlling input costs and meeting competitive product prices. In recent years, LOL has come to view animal feed as "information in a bag." Its competitive advantage lies not so much in the ability to shave input costs as in ensuring that its formulation of ingredients meets the current needs of livestock producers. LOL has shifted its view of feed production from that of Capital management to competitive use of Knowledge.

Making this shift of perspective is not simple. It necessarily involves an understanding of the organizational uses of information as well as an appreciation of the difference between information and Knowledge. In the paragraphs below, we'll try to take you through this shift by examining how corporations have historically used information and how they can come to view their reservoir of Knowledge as a corporate asset.

Information and Organization

The relationship between information and organization has been both long and intense. From the earliest times, records of transactions have made it possible for managers to control the day-to-day activities of purchasing, production and sales. Aggregated records provide measures of profitability and point to business opportunities which may materialize in the future. As Max Weber has noted, the modern organization cannot exist without information.

With the onset of computer-stored databases, the basic information-organization relationship has changed in several important ways. First, the capacity to store and process ever-larger volumes of information supports larger, more complex organizations. Second, the structure of organizational information can be analyzed to identify causal variables which enhance management's capacity to plan and control. Finally, and most importantly, a new type of employee, the "knowledge worker" has emerged to engage in a continuous dialog with the corporate database.

These developments have changed the role of organizational information. In the past, information has been used primarily for management control and performance monitoring. While these functions remain, they are beginning to take second place to a view of information as a corporate asset. This means that information has value and that investments in it can produce returns in the form of increased efficiency and expanded opportunity.

In this chapter, we explore the Knowledge Resource and how it can be used tactically to manage complex, distributed organization systems. We also address the strategic use of information for identifying new products and services and for the purpose of planning future activities. In each case, we make use of knowledge-organizing paradigms which help business men and women use and manage Knowledge.

The paradigms which direct the use of information in organizations have a special character; one that sets them apart from many of the paradigms we have been discussing. They are real in that the significant features of each paradigm are clearly observable in the structure of the organization or in the behavior of customers, employees and managers.

Consider, for instance, the general accounting paradigm which links money and product. This paradigm helps create a paper trail of the movement of product with specific documents mandated at given points in product flow. Orders initiate production; distributors are Invoiced for product and customers are Billed on delivery.

FIGURE 10.1

PRODUCTION AND ACCOUNTING:
A PARADIGM AT WORK

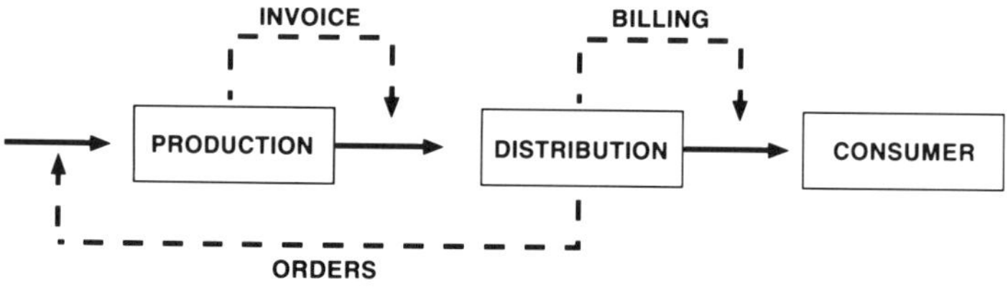

These relationships are clear in Figure 10.1 where product flow is represented by solid arrows and accounting information by dotted arrows. The accounting paradigm is not only easily observable in action, it is extremely powerful. So much so that it forces a division of labor in the organization between steps in the product flow as well as a set of practices which is virtually identical across organizations. The paradigm is so durable that it is taught to production managers and accountants and, in the latter case, constitutes the framework for professional certification examinations.

Such familiar business paradigms are not just a matter of academic interest. Nor are they to be taken for granted as the best way to structure business activity. Instead, we must view them as the result of historical development of business practice and question their viability in the new realities of the nineties. They are starting points for transforming the organization into new, ecologically-sound configurations and must, as a result, be foremost in management thinking.

As we work through our analysis of the Knowledge Resource, it's absolutely essential that readers stand back from our narrative and filter what we say through the lenses of current business paradigms. Paradigms transform information into Knowledge. If the corporation is to make use of knowledge, all managers and employees must have a clear understanding of the ruling paradigms which support their activities.

The Tactical Use of Information

This is a use of information which is familiar to most managers. It involves the basic records of the organization which support several key management functions as suggested by Figure 10.2.

FIGURE 10.2

TACTICAL USES OF ORGANIZATION INFORMATION

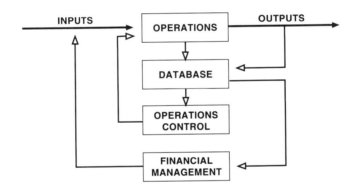

At the core of 10.2, we see that the flow of events in organization Operations produces a Database. This includes all purchases and sales as well as records of organization processes and use of resources. These data are used tactically in two major processes 1) Operations Control and 2) Financial Management.

1) Operations Control uses models of the production-sales process to access the database. The combination of database and models constitutes a decision-support system which assists managers in solving daily operational problems.

2) Financial Management uses standard financial models to assess the profitability of the organization. Managers use these models to reduce the operational records of the organization to a set of standard fiscal indicators which can be compared across organizations.

The tactical use of information depends upon these widely-held management models and paradigms. They dictate the types of information collected and the sorts of decision problems which can be addressed. As a result, the tactical objective for managers is:
IDENTIFY OPERATIONAL AND FINANCIAL PARADIGMS WHICH APPLY THE KNOWLEDGE RESOURCE TO EMERGING ORGANIZATIONAL PROCESSES.

Example: The 1980s have already proven the value of models for the tactical use of information. Spreadsheet software has made it possible for financial analysts to carry out complex fiscal studies in a coordinated fashion. Production management software has been integrated with office systems to effect complete, coordinated control over manufacturing operations.

These applications have, however, been driven by a general "linear system" production paradigm. This holds that design, engineering, manufacturing and marketing are steps in a sequential process. This results in long start-up times and a lack of responsiveness of the organization to market conditions.

The same decision support systems have recently been accessed by a new paradigm, that of "concurrent engineering." This paradigm throws over the old linear model of production in favor of an approach whereby the inputs of all major actors are considered throughout the design-development process. The results is increased responsiveness and substantial savings (Business Week, 1990).

The point of this example is that the tactical use of information is driven by paradigms. Most of these paradigms are drawn from the training and experience of managers, engineers and accountants. Accordingly, they are expressions of historical views of organization; they perpetuate the past.

Occasionally, a new paradigm comes along and causes a rethinking of old ideas and practices. Concurrent engineering is the case in point. By taking a new perspective on design and production, concurrent engineering reorganizes the whole product development process. It is, on a small scale, a new paradigm for production organizations.

The challenge to the modern manager is to be the master of existing paradigms while, at the same time, searching for new ways of viewing organization and process. Responding to this challenge requires complete understanding of current practice without rigid commitment to it. Then, new paradigms can be evaluated as to their capacity to solve organization problems.

What the "paradigm-sensitive" manager does, is look toward the anomalies which current paradigms are unable to address. This happens when a paradigm is pushed too far. As Masterman states, "It is not only the case that a fully-extended paradigm, or theory, reaches a point where the further extension of it produces diminishing returns. The situation is worse. The paradigm itself goes bad on you . . ." (Masterman, 1976).

A far-reaching example of one such "bad paradigm" is that of the stock vs. flow view of business operations. For decades, managers were able to direct their organizations by controlling stocks such as inventory, account balances, and orders. In the 1960s and 1970s, the stock paradigm proved to be ineffective under conditions of rapidly changing markets and evolving technology. Instead, managers were forced to turn to a flow paradigm which focused on cash, work in progress, and consumer preferences. This new paradigm effectively addressed many of the anomalies which were making life difficult for managers.

Responsiveness to paradigm failure and receptivity to new ideas is evidence of tactical maturity on the part of managers. They make full use of the Knowledge Resource in support of the daily work of the organiza-

FIGURE 10.3

**FROM TACTICS TO STRATEGY:
THE EVOLUTION OF THE KNOWLEDGE RESOURCE**

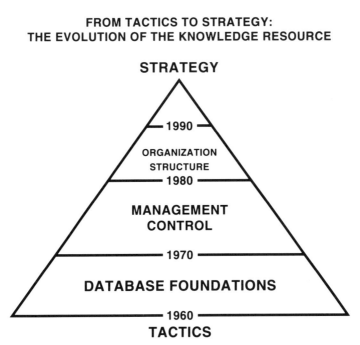

tion. They also set the stage for the strategic use of information to position the organization for the future.

The Strategic Use of Information

Strategic use of the Knowledge Resource is an evolutionary process. It is not independent of tactics, instead it builds them as suggested by Figure 10.3.

Figure 10.3 shows that the Resource is founded on the organization's Database as it developed through the decade of the 1970s. To this, we add the Management Controls of the eighties as described in our discussion of tactics.

Beginning with the 1990s, Knowledge takes on a Strategic character as it begins to support new Organization Structures. These innovations are made possible by the electronic communication of information (Fulk and Steinfeld, 1990). Thus, both the content of information and access to it become the defining dynamic of the organization of the nineties.

Information-based structural change takes two major forms. First, there is a geographic independence which fosters global dispersal of organization activities. Communications systems provide the "glue" which integrates production in Mexico with finance in New York under management in Tokyo. Second, there is a fluidity of organization which permits adaptation to changing environments. What this implies is that the modern knowledge worker is also a mobile resource which can be drawn from any number of locations to address specific organizational problems (See Fulk and Steinfeld, p. 275). The structural consequences of Knowledge management can be summarized in a second principle as:

MANAGERS SHOULD BRING THE KNOWLEDGE RESOURCE TO BEAR ON ORGANIZATION PROBLEMS BY USING COMMUNICATIONS TECHNOLOGY TO SUPPORT AND CONTROL KNOWLEDGE WORKERS.

There is a higher use of information strategy in this principle which has to do with information as knowledge. What we are referring to here, are the field-organizing paradigms used by corporate knowledge workers. Their paradigms relate Knowledge to larger field-specific databases outside the organization. As knowledge workers mesh these Resources, they identify new business opportunities and directions for organization development.

At present, the strategic use of Knowledge by organizations is unmanaged and left largely in the hands of individual knowledge workers. For instance, engineers are expected to be informed of developments in their respective fields and to apply them in the organization. In most organizations, this is viewed as an "after hours" assignment and no special provisions are made to support the engineer in his or her professional activities.

These practices are woefully inadequate for the business environment of the 2000s. Information will increasingly give way to knowledge and the successful organization will be the one that connects itself with the evolving fields in which it works. This means that those who manage knowledge workers must be aware of field-organizing paradigms and sensitive to paradigm shifts that signal the onset of new, more powerful problem-solving capacity. Along with management awareness of the corporate knowledge base, there needs to be a strategic commitment which allocates resources to the field-related activities of knowledge workers. MANAGERS MAINTAIN AND INCREASE THE STRATEGIC VALUE OF CORPORATE KNOWLEDGE BY PROVIDING FOR RELATIONSHIPS BETWEEN IT AND FIELD-SPECIFIC KNOWLEDGE.

In the pyramid of Figure 10.3, we show that the year 2000 is a time when Knowledge strategy will assume primary importance. This proposition suggests that the primary strategic concern is to transform information into Knowledge. Managers and knowledge workers are challenged to use their imaginations to build upon the knowledge base of the organization. By continually searching for new uses of Knowledge, they will not only promote the vitality of the organization, they will also add to its foundation of Knowledge.

Managing Paradigms

So far in this book, we've been talking about the effect of paradigms on business leaders. We've shown how their thinking and actions are determined by the myths, models and metaphors they use to organize their experience. The reader should recognize that the arguments used to support these conclusions hold just as well for knowledge workers within the corporation. Each group of workers and each set of professionals has its "ruling paradigm" which shapes the thought and action of each individual. Thus, if organizations are to make use of Knowledge, managers must be aware of the key paradigms which support their business ventures. And, they must manage paradigms to ensure that the organization makes use of relevant knowledge in a timely fashion.

The core concepts in any business paradigm are found in the everday language of researchers and practitioners. No problem solving or research is possible without a consensus as to the meanings of these concepts and knowledge about how they are related to one another. When an electrical engineer sits at a workstation to design a new microchip, he or she has a set of concepts in mind which give him or her access to the knowledge needed to develop the design. Because these concepts and their relationships are well known, it is relatively easy to carry out the design task and to communicate its features to fellow engineers. They share a professional paradigm.

This example makes very good sense. Managers of organizations in the electronics business wouldn't think of employing people who were unaware of the microelectronics paradigm. They also would not be comfortable with engineers who failed to keep in touch with new developments in the field. Yet, many of these very same managers find themselves at a loss when they think about managing the professional activities of knowledge workers. Managers find it difficult to manage paradigms because they have no convenient way to think about them and no way to determine whether their employees are in touch with developments in their fields.

Although we recognize the difficulty involved in the leap from people management to paradigm management, we take the position that this is not only possible, it is necessary. Managers can move in this direction by considering how professional paradigms are formed and how they are used to solve business problems. This can be accomplished by directing management attention to the ways professional knowledge is stored and accessed (Ammentorp and Johnson, 1989). In Chapter 3, we described the process whereby professionals are linked to their knowledge via shared paradigms. Let's take a closer look at the inner workings of these links.

In recent years, the literature of most professions has become accessible through computer-stored text databases. These databases contain reports of the work of researchers and practitioners indexed by key words. The catalog of key words for any one of these databases is the working list of concepts shared by all those who practice in the field.

Practitioners in the information sciences have recognized this property of text databases for some time. They have used analyses of document similarity to develop search strategies (Griffiths, et.al., 1986), and hierarchical analyses to structure entire databases (Lee, 1981). In these applications, it is the associations among concepts which constitute the underlying structure of the field. In fact, without some such knowledge-organizing structure, professional use of text databases is impossible (Smith and Genesereth, 1985).

The contributions of these approaches to our management problem lies in the notion of key word association. Simply put, the extent to which two key words co-occur in the database is a measure of the extent to which they belong to the same higher-level concept. Thus, when our electrical engineer associates the words "NAND" AND "NOR," he or she is working within the concept of "logic gate" at the very foundation of circuit design. If our engineer uses these key words to access the field database, he or she will obtain a large set of references to the use of these "gates" in circuit design. He or she will, of course, need to quickly move to a more specific level of key words so that the results of his or her search will be useful.

The information flows associated with the professional use of data bases are shown in Figure 10.4 (reproduced from Figure 3.1).

FIGURE 10.4

PARADIGM AND KNOWLEDGE USE IN THE PROFESSIONS

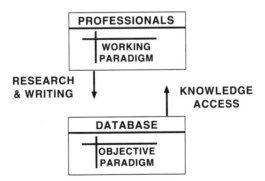

In this drawing, the two paradigms are represented by the co-occurrence of key words. The "Objective Paradigm" is what we would find if we simply looked to the ways key words appear in entries in the database. The "Working Paradigm" is found in the ways professionals associate key words in their everyday speech and in the ways they use key words to access the database. At any point in time, the "ruling paradigm" is the pattern of key word association used by the majority of professionals in the field.

What's important about Figure 10.4, is that the two paradigms are constantly changing. As Researchers and Practitioners use knowledge, they discover new concepts and new relationships which alter the Objective Paradigm when they are added to the database. As these new findings and concepts become known to the profession, they bring about changes in the Working Paradigm. As a result, professional knowledge is dynam-

FIGURE 10.5
TELECOMMUNICATIONS PARADIGM

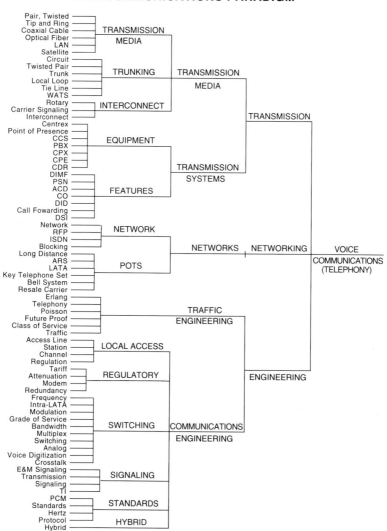

ic and every user must be able to track paradigm evolution in order to access new ideas and practices.

Let's look at a more detailed example to see how a "ruling paradigm" shapes the use of knowledge in a field. Telecommunications is an instance of an exploding technology where new concepts are invented by the minute. If professionals are unable to fit these concepts into a Working Paradigm, they will not be able to make efficient use of telecommunications knowledge. To address this management problem, the authors examined the associations among the words most frequently used by telecommunications professionals. The structure shown in Figure 10.5 is a "map" of the telecommunications knowledge base.

Here we have, for the first time, an actual picture of a paradigm. This "tree" aggregates the basic concepts of telecommunications in a hierarchical structure. On the left-hand side of the diagram, all terms are unique; they are the raw material from which the paradigm is constructed. As we move to the right, these concepts come together in higher-order clusters until, at the right-hand side, all concepts are placed in the same group.

This structure becomes a paradigm when labels are assigned to the branches of the tree. For instance, the top five words in Figure 10.5: "Pair-Twisted . . . LAN" are associated under the higher-order concept "Transmission Medium." This concept then goes together with "Trunking" and "Interconnect" to make up the next level concept "Transmission Media" and so on.

By "taking a picture" of a paradigm, we can make use of knowledge in several important ways. First, visual representation of paradigms serve as guides to knowledge workers. They can more effectively search their databases and they are less likely to miss connections among key concepts. Second, higher-order concepts in the paradigm are indicators of relationships among sub-fields in the profession. Thus, "Transmission" points to the integration of "Media" and "Systems." By following this map, professionals and managers can ensure communications among specialties so that knowledge is shared. Finally, the identification of specialties by higher-order concepts gives form to training in the field. It also identifies bodies of information which managers should consider in hiring new employees.

Can paradigms be managed? In the past, managers dealt with the use of knowledge in the corporation by hiring people with appropriate specialties. They then left the issues of knowlege use and paradigm change to these professionals. It's our contention that the manager of the nineties cannot deal with the explosive growth of knowledge in this way. Instead, he or she will need to create a system for knowledge access and use in the organization along with a set of procedures for monitoring paradigm change. Then, the most current knowledge can be brought to bear on solving operational problems and developing innovative products and services.

Paradigm management is, of course, in its infancy. However, there are several guidelines which managers can follow to support their knowledge workers. These represent an expansion of the general principles noted above. They include:

1) Develop a Knowledge Worker Support System (KWSS) which gives each professional access to timely information.

In the KWSS, each knowledge worker has a workstation with computer and communication capabilities which link him or her to appropriate databases and to other professionals in the corporation. These workstations must follow the general principles of socio-technical design so that each knowledge worker is drawn into the corporate network of professionals (Chorafas, 1985). At the same time, the connection of this workstation to the outside world gives the knowledge worker access to specialized databases and facilitates his or her communication with other professionals.

2) Visualize the ruling paradigm in each professional specialty.

This does not mean that managers must be experts in all fields. What it implies is that managers encourage professionals to think about the knowledge-organizing paradigms in their fields. It should be possible, for example, for any professional to draw a simplified version of Figure 10.5 which can serve as a reference point for discussions with managers.

The visualization of paradigms will, unfortunately, be a difficult task for most knowledge workers. Paradigms are not taught in most professional schools; they are learned by experience and rarely reduced to a diagram. Accordingly, managers will have to take the lead in the visualization task and hone their conceptual skills in order to help knowledge workers come to grips with the structure of their fields.

3) Identify the potential for paradigm shifts and support them when they occur.

For many knowledge workers, paradigm development does not continue beyond "basic training." Knowledge structures developed by professionals in colleges and universities remain firmly in place throughout entire careers. This is, of course, a disabling characteristic in fields where major paradigm shifts are taking place. And, it is probably the most critical paradigm management task facing business leaders in the 1990s.

Managers can view this task as a need to "unfreeze" the ways their knowledge workers approach the subject matter of their fields. If Step (2) has been carried out and professionals have a shared paradigm in place, managers can begin to probe for areas of weakness where new knowledge is needed. This can sensitize knowledge workers to the potential for paradigm shift and stimulate them to active search for new developments in the knowledge base.

Despite the difficulty involved in tracking paradigm change, managers should pursue this task vigorously. This is where new technology can be discovered and transformed into business opportunity for the organization.

On Imagination

Paradigm management is the way business leaders put the message of this book to work in their organizations. By thinking about paradigms and the meanings they give to information, managers are able to tap the knowledge resource and identify corporate opportunity. But they can't access opportunity by restricting innovation and binding their organizations to past practice. They must take risks and imagine new paradigms and support the innovations needed to reap their benefits.

The exercise of imagination is not a simple task. Old paradigms die hard. They are rooted in the ways we see business activity and they are supported by countless beliefs and practices. When they are challenged, they fight back and often submerge the imaginative with the mundane. They also induce loyalty by making everything familiar and all actions routine. Consequently, imagination and leadership are closely bound up. Business leaders must be able to imagine the potential in paradigm shifts and draw on their leadership skills to make them a reality.

References

Ammentorp, W. and Johnson, M. (1989) *The Definition and Diffusion of Professional Paradigms*. Paper presented at annual meeting, American Educational Research Association. San Francisco, CA.

Anthony, R. (1965) *Planning and Control Systems*. Cambridge, MA: Harvard University Press.

Chorafas, D. (1985) *Management Workstations for Greater Productivity.* New York: McGraw Hill.

Chubin, D. and Hackett, E. (1990) *Peerless Science.* Albany, NY: State University of New York Press.

"Concurrent Engineering" (1990) *Business Week*, April 30, p. 110.

Diebold, J. (1985) *Business in the Age of Information.* New York: American Management Association.

Emery, J. (1969) *Organizational Planning and Control Systems.* New York: Macmillan.

Fulk, J. and Stanfield, C. (eds) (1990) *Organizations and Communication Technology.* Newbury Park, CA: Sage.

Griffiths, A. et.al. (1986) "Using Interdocument Similarity Information in Document Retrieval Systems," *Journal of the American Society for Information Science* 37(1).

Hax, A. and Maljuf, N. (1984) *Strategic Management.* Englewood Cliffs, NJ: Prentice Hall.

Hinton, R. (1988) *Information Technology and How to Use It.* Cambridge, England: ICSA Publishing Co.

Lee, R. (1981) "Cluster Analysis and Its Applications," In Tou (ed) *Advances in Information Systems Science*, Vol 8. New York: Plenum.

Marx, P. (1987) "The Legal Risks of Using Information as a Competitive Weapon," *Information Management Review* 2(4).

Masterman, M. (1976) The Nature of a Paradigm. In Lakatos and Musgrave (eds) *Criticism and the Growth of Knowledge.* London: Cambridge University Press.

Porter, M. (1980) *Competitive Strategy.* New York: Free Press.

Price, D. (1986) *Little Science—Big Science.* New York: Columbia University Press.

Simon, H. (1977) *The New Science of Management Decision.* Englewood Cliffs, NJ: Prentice Hall.

Smith, D. and Genesereth, M. (1985) "Ordering Conjunctive Queries," *Artificial Intelligence* 26(2).

Synott, W. and Gruber, W. (1981) *Information Resource Management.* New York: J. Wiley.

Wiseman, C. (1988) *Strategic Information Systems.* Homewood, IL: Irwin.

CHAPTER 11

The Imagination Dynamic

ORGANIZATION	ALTERNATIVE PARADIGMS		
DIMENSION	COMMUNIST	CAPITALIST	TRANSFORMAL
DYNAMIC	Ideology	Entrepreneur-ship	Imagination

Paradigms and their driving forces—Dynamics—are inseparable. They bring together the functional determinants of human behavior—the Paradigm—with the psychic energy of people—the Dynamic. When these two dimensions of organization life are both present, business activity is likely to be successful. When one or both are absent, business is without focus and at risk of failure.

The link between Paradigm and Dynamic is especially important for business leaders in the turbulent environment of the nineties. The Transformal Paradigm provides structures for business activity and marshalls the resources needed to compete in a global marketplace. Imagination gives this Paradigm the motivating force required to continually adapt the organization to its environment.

Business without paradigm is confusion.

Business without imagination is delusion.

(DeThomasis, 1990)

Throughout this book, we've presented the Transformal Paradigm as a set of metaphors and models which business women and men can use to lead their organizations. Now, we need to infuse these constructs with the Imagination Dynamic to energize the adaptive capacity of the organization. To do this, we'll concentrate on the images business leaders use to construct a mental picture of the organization and a vision of what it might become. This is what has defined successful leadership in the past and it is what will determine who will manage viable businesses in the future.

Down through history the determining factor between leaders who were effective and leaders who were not has been the acuity of perception. Those leaders who chose to utilize their imagination and creativity have gone forward while those who relied on their power and dominance have not (Anthony, et.al., 1988, p. 105).

These are the people we called Paradigmers in Chapter 10; those who are masters of the ruling paradigms in their organizations. They are also the Paradigm Breakers who are able to see the need for new business metaphors and models; women and men who have the insight to anticipate change and the courage to initiate it.

Metaphor and Imagination

Creative use of the Imagination Dynamic rests on the ability of business leaders to visualize their organizations in efficient, flexible ways. To be efficient, these visions must summarize wide ranges of organization behavior in meaningful terms. Leaders must have a clear picture of the forces which control business activity along with the points where management interventions can bring about desired changes. Visions must be flexible so that business leaders can see new organizational configurations readily. Flexibility allows business men and women to conduct mental explorations of alternative future scenarios; it unleashes creativity.

The primary visualization aid is the metaphor. It concretizes thought and helps business leaders share their visions with others. As Morgan notes:

> Images and metaphors are not only interpretive constructs or ways of seeing; they also provide frameworks for action. Their use creates insights that often allow us to act in ways that we may not have thought possible before (1986, p. 343).

What Morgan is saying is that useful metaphors must also conform to the standards of efficiency and flexibility. In addition, they are frameworks for action. By sharing metaphors, all members of the organization have a frame of reference which can inform their decisions and link insights to action.

To see how a metaphor can help us unleash the Imagination Dynamic, let's think of the organization as nuclear reactor. This is a metaphor which incorporates most of the features of the Transformal Paradigm discussed in earlier chapters. It also emphasizes the use of organizational energy to cope with environmental demand.

Productivity Pellets: The fuel for our organizational reactor is packaged in small activity units or "Productivity Pellets" where the technology used by the organization interacts with the corporate knowledge base. We picture these "Pellets" as tiny spheres enclosing the energy exchanges involved in the technology-knowledge relationship.

FIGURE 11.1

PRODUCTIVITY PELLETS

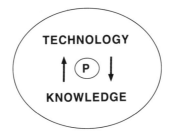

A simple example of such a "Pellet" would be a work processing station in manufacturing. In modern production systems, these are already designated as "cells" where the technology of production is controlled by knowledge in the form of computer programs (Ammentorp, 1986). Production "cells" are designed to carry out specific operations and are able to act autonomously within their design limits. Thus, a numerically-controlled machine can accept work from outside its "cell," perform any programmed operation on it and pass it along to another "cell." Hence, the over-all Productivity of the system is determined by the Productivities of its constituent "Pellets."

A better example for our purposes is that of the workstation. In workstation "Pellets," knowledge workers interact with information technology to carry out clerical and/or conceptual tasks (Simon, 1977). Computing and imaging technologies are used by Knowledge workers to configure information for processing by the workstation. In effect, the "Pellet" receives information from outside the workstation, takes action on that information, and passes the results to other workstations in the organization.

This is a good example as it puts imagination at the root of organizational energy. The imaging technologies of workstations enable knowledge workers to see the work of the organization from different perspectives. This facilitates the creative process and gives the Imagination Dynamic free rein to test new ideas and practices which may help the organization better adapt to its environment.

This example illustrates another key feature of the "Pellets." The larger organization deals with each "Pellet" in terms of the inputs it provides and the outputs it receives. The organization need not be concerned with the internal workings of each "Pellet." In fact, "Pellets" have considerable autonomy as to their modes of operation so long as they fulfill their role in the organizational workflow. Each "Pellet" has the capacity to innovate and to seek out the most efficient ways to perform its task.

Fueling Business: In any complex organization, the individual units or "Pellets" cannot stand alone. They must exchange work, resources and information with one another. These exchanges cannot be conducted on an ad hoc basis; they must be organized and controlled if the organization is to engage in any but the most simple tasks.

We've accommodated the problem of exchange coordination and control in our metaphor by creating "Business Fuel Rods" which are collections of "Productivity Pellets."

Each "Fuel Rod" can be thought of as a business line which processes inputs into products and services. These outputs can be used by other "Rods" in the organization, or passed along to the marketplace.

FIGURE 11.2

BUSINESS FUEL RODS

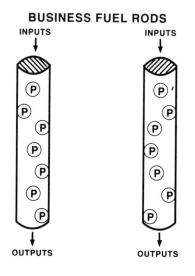

In our metaphor, the "Pellets" in a given "Rod" are never at rest. Their interactions are continually reconfigured to improve the input-output flows through the "Rod." This provides a second source of flexibility in the metaphor as each "Rod" is constrained only by its position in the over-all input-output dynamics of the organization. How the "Rod" deals with throughput is determined internally; the larger organization simply sets the boundaries on flows between "Rods."

Again, our metaphor emphasizes autonomy. Decisions within business line "Rods" are only generally constrained by organization goals. Thus, "Rods" truly fuel the organization in that they generate and focus energy on throughput tasks. They are not passive processors of activity or product flow; they shape that flow in accord with corporate constraints and objectives. Thus, an environment is created that fosters creativity and innovation without disrupting the necessary exchanges needed to "run" the organization.

The Corporate Reactor: Corporations are energized by their constituent businesses. By bringing businesses together, corporations pursue the Value-generation goal we described in Chapter 9. The focusing of corporate energy can be visualized in our metaphor by the Corporate Reactor as pictured in Figure 11.3.

Here we see the aggregation of several business "Rods" in the "reactor box." The performance of the "reactor" is indicated on the "value meter"

FIGURE 11.3

THE CORPORATE REACTOR

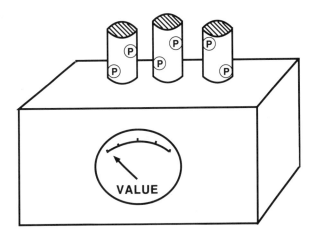

on its face. The relative contribution of each "Rod" to Value generation is represented by the extent to which it is emerged in the "Reactor." That is, businesses with heavy contributions to the corporation are more deeply emerged in the "Reactor" and those peripheral to the corporation are withdrawn.

The reactor metaphor also helps business leaders imagine corporate synergy. As business lines, "Rods," react in the core of the corporation, they can produce more total Value than they might as separate entities. These businesses benefit from corporate leadership and are able to take advantage of parallel activities in other business lines. This is true "reaction" in that energy is released which would be otherwise contained within each business line.

The performance of several business lines depends on how well the corporation deals with its environment. In the Reactor metaphor, this appears as "load balancing." If we think of the Reactor as generating electric power for input to a grid which links it to other generators and users, we can visualize how "load balancing" works. As demand and generation change, the individual Reactor needs to be carefully managed to ensure that it makes its appropriate contribution to the grid without destroying itself or its loads. The same can be said of the corporation; it too must balance its environmental "loads" in order to keep its Value performance at a maximum.

There is a darker side to this metaphor. That is the "China Syndrome" or the "Chernobyl Meltdown" where the Reactor runs out of control. In the Corporate Reactor, this is uncontrolled business growth which may give the illusion of success while, in fact, generating negative cash flows. As Hammermesh points out, the business lines within the Corporate Reactor must each be tuned to the proper "load" in order to realize growth potential within cash flow limits that enhance over-all corporate Value generation (1986). The operative word here is "tuned." It helps us imagine business leaders as "corporate engineers" who continually monitor environmental load as demand and market share, energy flow in the form of cash, and performance as measured by corporate Value generation.

From Metaphor to Model

Metaphor, you will recall, is only one part of paradigm. As paradigms become widely used, they produce a reservoir of experience and knowledge which is organized into models. In modern organizations, these models are increasingly formal and often cast in the form of computer programs to

FIGURE 11.4

VISUALIZING ORGANIZATION

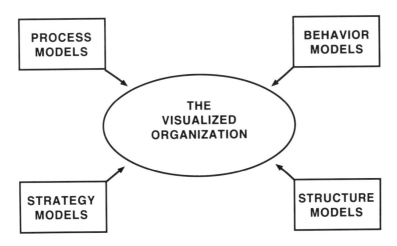

assist in the design and management of complex processes. It is, in many cases, impossible to carry out business activities without the use of such models and managers who ignore them do so at considerable risk.

What models do is set a framework for the exercise of imagination. They provide a concrete foundation for visualizing the multiplicity of activities in the corporation. In Figure 11.4, we suggest how four types of corporate models feed into the imagination of business leaders.

Each of these collections of models is representative of a relatively well-known aspect of organizational behavior. As business women and men consider their organizations, models help them identify variables and relationships which must be incorporated in any viable future scenario. The contribution of models to the visualizing process is easy to see in the following examples.

Process Models: Every business organization has a core technology which organizes workflow to convert inputs of energy and materials into outputs of goods and services. Core technologies are made up of causal relationships which specify the consequences of actions taken during the conversion process. Refineries, for instance, are completely determined by the chemical reactions which convert crude oil into market products. Steel mills are similarly structured by the physical steps involved in changing raw ingots into finished product. Even the human services have regular steps whereby clients are educated, healed or otherwise cared for.

Insofar as managers are concerned, basic Processes need to be controlled. Inputs and outputs must be coordinated and matched to market demand. Models make this possible by representation of process dynamics in ways that permit accurate prediction of the effects of management action (Lyneis, 1982). This is usually done in computer simulations where managers can determine what happens to workflow and process activities given assumptions about market conditions and control policies. Simulations are powerful visualization aids as they enable managers to reduce complex processes to their bare essentials. In effect, the core activities of the organization are pictured as graphic simulation output. This frees management imagination and gives business men and women the opportunity to experiment with alternative actions without risk to the organization.

Behavior Models: People are, of course, the essential ingredient in any organization. It follows that managers must be able to visualize the behavior patterns of individuals and groups and the variables which determine how these patterns will evolve over time. Models are particularly helpful in this case, because human behavior is only partly predictable and controllable only in a general sense. By accessing Behavior Models, managers can reduce some of the uncertainties of organizational behavior and, at the same time, identify those policies and actions which are likely to shape behavior to desired ends.

Although Behavior Models are not so precise as their Process counterparts, recent advances in modeling technique have made it possible to represent many of the social and psychological aspects of organizational life. Issues such as worker burnout have been the subject of simulation studies in which evidence gathered in research and experience goes to creating a model which can illuminate the causal structure underlying the behavior of interest (Homer, 1985).

Behavior Models are especially useful in imaging the organization. They take what is normally a complex, confusing problem and reduce it to its essential elements. They give business leaders the capacity to include human resources in their visioning of organization futures. By adding the human equation, these models enrich the imagination of managers and improve the quality of the decisions they make.

Structure Models: The modern corporation is organized by the communication links which bind its business activities into a working whole. Modern information technology, it is argued, has significantly changed the form of the corporation, its modes of action and the ways it uses resources (Huber, 1989). These developments give business leaders an increased array of options as to how the corporation is to be structured in pursuit of its objectives.

The structural alternatives available to business men and women of the nineties are sufficiently complex that they cannot be easily visualized. They can be understood only through the medium of simulation models of the underlying communications systems (Garrison, 1985). These Structure Models are different from all other Models in Figure 11.4; they are isomorphic to the actual communication systems of the organization. They are able to carry out "real time" simulations of information flow so that they can be used to design communication networks and select the equipment needed for their implementation. As such, they are powerful visualization tools which give business leaders a "working picture" of organization structure.

Structure Models also unlock the imagination of business men and women. Through their graphic output, these Models permit the user to see the organization in action. This makes the Model a design "work-bench" where business leaders can imagine alternative structures and put them to an immediate test. Consequently, they play a much more important role than that of models in earlier business paradigms. In traditional paradigms, models were coercive and served to limit the thinking of managers to a certain set of standard organizational configurations. In contrast, modern Structure Models are liberating; they encourage the imagination of new structures which can be tested through simulation before they are put in place in the corporation.

Strategy Models: Of all the models available to business leaders, Strategy Models are perhaps the most widely used. During the 1980s, researchers and executives discovered that the Value of an organization could be directly traced to certain of the operating parameters of its business lines. Studies by the Strategic Planning Institute showed that 70% of the variability in corporate bottom line performance could be accounted for by 30 key strategic variables (Buzzell and Gale, 1987). These variables are located in the financial and marketing records of the organization and can be readily aggregated into Strategic Models of corporate operations.

Due to the close linkage of Strategic Models and the day-to-day working financial models of the corporation, these Models help bring strategic thinking down to the operational level of the organization. They translate the "what if" questions imagined by business leaders into the dollars and cents of corporate performance. Strategic Models also facilitate action on imagined new directions by altering the use of resources in the organization. In effect, an imagined direction is tested by a "what if" question in the Model which points to appropriate changes in resource use.

Strategic Models are important aids to imagination in another way. Since most such Models are based on the aggregate performance of corporations throughout an industry, business leaders are able to compare their imagined futures with industry standards. For example, industry returns on spending for research might be high. This would stimulate the Strategic Modeler to test the impact of greater research activity in his or her own organization. By continually subjecting management thinking to the test of industry performance, Strategic Models "jog" the imagination of business women and men and help prevent the stagnation of business as usual.

The Transformation of Organization: In Search of Butterflies

There's a story we like to tell to illustrate the mind set of the Transformal Leader. It goes something like this. Once there were four children who were asked to participate in a psychological experiment to test their powers of imagination. The psychologist showed the children a room filled with sacks, straw and other litter and asked them to tell what they saw. The three boys in the experiment, let's call them Cohen, March and Olsen agreed that the room was filled with useless garbage. The girl, let's call her Mary Kay, immediately rushed into the room and pawed through the litter saying over and over again, "There must be a butterfly in here somewhere!"

The point of this story is not that the Transformal Leader has delusions of turning garbage into a thing of beauty. It's more subtle than that. What the story says is that viewing the organization as a "garbage can" filled with political interest groups points only to an erratic, hopeless future. While an optimistic imagination can see the transformation of the mundane into a new form. It also points to the fact that there are those whose views limit the imagination; this is the "garbage can" metaphor of Cohen, March and Olsen (1972). And, quite the opposite, there are those like Mary Kay Ash who have founded entirely new organizations which have created value and opportunity for countless individuals. (Ash, 1987)

We don't, however, mean that the politics of organizations can be ignored. It is a fact of life, but it may be only one type of organization along some continuum of alternatives like that shown in Figure 11.5.

This drawing, taken, in modified form, from Mintzberg, is meant to suggest that there are several evolutionary paths open to the organization

FIGURE 11.5

THE ORGANIZATIONAL LIFE CYCLE

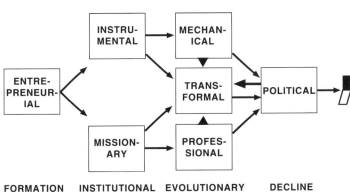

(Mintzberg, 1989, Figure 14-3, p. 283). Organizations which begin with an Entrepreneurial thrust can take any one of four routes as they mature. If the Entrepreneur succeeds, he or she must create a larger, more complex organization. It may be Instrumental in that routines become the central dynamic and bureaucracy the mode of control. The organization may move to a Missionary configuration as the original Entrepreneurial spirit becomes institutionalized.

Once the Institutional form has been created, the organization is faced with its most critical development options. The Instrumental organization can continue as a Mechanical entity where all activity is channelled and creativity is submerged by procedures and rules. Others can cast their Mission into a Professional environment where the larger world of professional life has a good deal to say about organization activity. Either of these basic Institutional forms also have the option to move to the Transformal configuration we've been describing in this book.

At this point in development, all organizations have the Transformal option open to them. Those which have become Transformal can continue to visualize new futures which will keep them viable over time. Both Mechanistic and Professional organizations can become Transformal by allowing the butterflies of opportunity emerge from the cocoons of maladaptive structure. And, once transformed, they can continue to vitalize themselves to remain in an Evolutionary state indefinitely.

One of the key lessons in Figure 11.5 is that Evolution leads ultimately to the grave (as Mintzberg's tombstone suggests). If nothing is done to initiate the Transformal process, all organizations will ultimately become

Political entities. They will emerge from their Evolution with sharp internal divisions of power and control which become the primary dynamic—driving all decisions and actions. Once this occurs, the organization loses its sense of mission and is truly unable to respond to its environment. It will ultimately die.

It is, therefore, the task of the transformal leader to keep his or her organization in an Evolutionary mode. He or she must be continually sensitive to the pressures which might move the organization to one of the unwanted configurations. In particular, there must be an unwavering opposition to the politicization of organizational life. If these sensibilities are not in the forefront of leadership, the organization is doomed to a death of the spirit and, in the longer run, disappearance from the business scene.

Faith and Finance: The Spirit of Organization

Up to this point, we've emphasized the rational side of paradigms. Much of our case for paradigm shifts rests on the reasonableness of new metaphors and the validity of their associated models of organizational behavior. In our arguments, mythology has played a minor role when it has surfaced at all. We're now at the stage in our discussion where we can no longer sit on the two-legged stool of metaphor and models; we must explore the mythology of management and the spiritual side of organization. There are two reasons why this is essential.

The first is pragmatic. Faith and finance are necessarily bound together in creating organizational futures where the human condition can flourish. As we've noted elsewhere:

> Finance, as the symbol of society's socioeconomic framework, pays the way for us, today, to manipulate, to control, and to change our own biological genetic substance; or to carry out collective self-destruction by interacting with the elementary building blocks of our world; or to create a worldwide communication and information network never imagined before; or to throw off the shackles of our own planet as men and women reach out to the rest of the universe. We can no longer live with the fantasy that this power, which in essence buys our future, can be void of the very faith of the men and women who must pay the price for this new creative power (DeThomasis, 1987, p. 6).

The relationship of this idea to our previous metaphor is that finance and its power to shape the future predisposes our "organizational reactor" to "core meltdowns" of inhuman proportions if left to itself. There must be countervailing faith in the potential for a workable ecological balance among the forces of production, individual interest and global carrying capacity. This integration of faith and finance is the key to liberation of the creative power of business and, at the same time, the essential limit on its possible misuse. For it is only in the whole that the true power of organization can be harnessed for the benefit of all people.

As deChardin sees it, the energy flowing through organization is "free." It has no necessary direction, but can follow the dictates of the human spirit.

> The vast industrial and social system in which we are enveloped does not threaten to crush us, neither does it seek to rob us of our soul. The energy emanating from it is free not only in the sense that it represents forces that can be used; it is moreover free because, in the whole no less than in the least of its elements, it arises in a state that is ever more spiritualized (deChardin, 1977).

This is the essence of our second rationale for examining the spiritual side of organization. There is a "spirit" residing in all organized activity; an idea that is generally accepted by many business leaders but only rarely articulated with any clarity. It is clear, for instance, that the inspirational literature of management has a spiritual foundation. It frequently speaks of deeper levels of understanding and meaning in interpersonal relationships that can only be spiritual in the final analysis. Fortunately, there are currents in this stream of thought which give more explicit visibility to the spiritual aspects of organizational behavior.

Spirit appears most clearly in the concept of organizational culture. There, myth and ritual empower the members of the organization toward collective accomplishments which cannot be achieved by a profane mechanism. Consider Harrison Owen's comment on how these "spirits" help to transform the organization.

> The role of myths and rituals in organization transformation is critical, for they shape and form the culture, which in turn provides the power, purpose and values of the organization (Owen, 1987).

There are many well-known examples of the impetus of spirit. These examples usually take on the attributes of collective commitment like that epitomized by the Data General employees to the *Soul of a New Machine* they were building (Kidder, 1981). In these examples, there is generally a nearly religious dimension to the individual's belief in the anticipated outcomes of organized activity. There is a faith that they can be attained and, usually, a charismatic leadership which mobilizes the beliefs and contributions of all members of the organization.

The Transformal Organization

In the previous six chapters of this book, we've defined what the transformal organization is and what it is not. We've also pointed to some of the changes that need to be made to present day business organizations to bring them into line with the Transformal Paradigm. And, we have identified some of the leadership skills needed to make the necessary changes. As we see it, imagination is the driving force which can give leaders the vision of the transformal organization.

Imagined views of organizational futures cannot, of course, be realized without a special kind of leadership. This involves the melding of rational problem-solving skills with insightful analyses of the social psychology of organizational behavior. But, these skills alone will not guarantee the transformation of the organization. They must go hand in hand with imagination and they require an infusion of spiritual energy if they are to excite the creativity of all employees and managers. It is a charismatic imagination which enables an organization to perceive alternative

FIGURE 11.6

THE TRANSFORMAL VISION

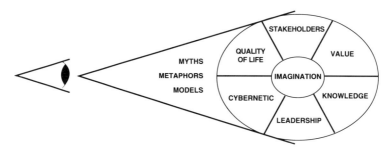

paradigms; to create visions of new organizational forms; to focus resources and energy on the transforming process.

The charismatic imagination uses the lens of paradigm, with its myths, metaphors and models, to extract a vision of the possible from the facts of organizational life. It is through the eyes of the charismatic leader that the transformal organization begins to take shape.

In Figure 11.6, we show how the leader's eye can see an organization in its transformal dimensions. In this drawing, we've put Imagination at the center to suggest its capacity to influence all aspects of organizational activity. As the leader envisions the transformal organization, he or she can draw on some general principles to assist in realizing the future. We have taken these from some of the major policy documents of our time in the hope that business women and men will imagine how human concerns can take the place of bottom line management. This is a transformation of the corporate imagination toward a "top line" approach to management where people count first and profits follow (DeThomasis, 1989). In the paragraphs below, we list these by way of summary of the message of this book.

Transforming Purpose: There is a compelling rational argument in the ecological literature that there is no future for organizations that fail to see Purpose in ecological terms. This fundamental truth is captured in the notion of Quality of Life as the Purpose of all organizations. It is the central theme of an emerging literature which emphasizes the critical condition of most of humankind. In these writings, it is poverty, health and access to opportunity which determine the Quality of Life of all people (United Nations, 1991). This idea becomes visionary when leaders themselves believe that it is possible to improve global quality of life. It becomes an ingredient of the leader's charisma when he or she articulates its spiritual overtones with organizational practice. This imaginative notion is at the center of the recent Papal *Encyclical* where Pope John Paul II states, "Development must not be understood solely in economic terms, but in a way that is fully human. It is not only a question of raising all peoples to the level currently enjoyed by the richest countries, but rather of building up a more decent life through united labor, of concretely enhancing every individual's dignity and creativity" (p. 13).

Transforming Stakeholders: This dimension can also be rationalized; organizations cannot prosper unless they take the interests of all Stakeholders into account. Markets shrink, workers are rebellious and communities are hostile if their Stakeholder interests are not considered by organizational leaders. This point of view is, however, too narrow and only serves to help the organization survive. To make it prosper, there must be a charism which advocates for Stakeholders. The least of their interests must find its way to the deliberations of organizational policy makers and it must be presented as equal in importance to the most weighty of other issues. In effect, the charismatic leader takes a measure of his or her credibility from a capacity to see the effects of organization on all Stakeholders.

For the Transformal Organization, the central Stakeholder concerns are those of workers. As the organization becomes increasingly dependent on technology, there is a danger that workers will be reduced to another form of "input" and that they will lose their identity and their capacity to contribute. This is the fundamental failing of socialism; by ignoring the humanity of workers, it failed to speak to the overpowering stake each has in his or her identity. To quote Pope John Paul II again, "It cannot be forgotten that the fundamental crisis of systems claiming to express the rule and indeed the dictatorship of the working class began with the great upheavals which took place in Poland in the name of solidarity. It was the throngs of working people which foreswore the ideology which presumed to speak in their name" (1991, page 10).

Transforming Value: This is the most analytic of the transformal dimensions. It has a substantial history in financial management and is understood by many—if not most—managers. Where charisma is needed is in holding to Value as the measure of organizational performance. This involves the confidence of leadership in Value production over the longer run and the ability to resist the pressure of short-run measures. It is a projection of the imagined future into the financial data of the organization by a leader who can argue "by the numbers."

The role of imagination in the search for Value lies in the word "future." The transformal leader must be able to see a course for organization development where cash flows can be increased; this can only be accomplished by pursuing Value rather than quarterly profit-loss balances. The importance of a focus on Value cuts across all types of organizations and economic systems. It assures the future for the Madison Avenue firm and guarantees the liberation of the economically disadvantaged in the poorest developing nation (Truitt, 1991).

Transforming the Cybernetic: There can be little argument with the proposition that all organizations are increasingly information driven. However, most are truly "driven" in that they follow the developments of information technology and do not lead them. Here is where informed charisma is absolutely essential. Only those organizations which take leadership in the use of information technology will be competitive in the global marketplace. Thus, the charismatic leader must have a vision of that market which links his or her organization to world-wide information networks in responsive ways.

Transforming Knowledge: If business leaders recognize the importance of Knowledge in the organization of the future, they will access a resource which has its own internal capacity to transform. Knowledge is by nature dynamic and it would seem that the organization need only keep up to date if it is to use this resource productively. We hope that readers of this book recognize that this is a narrow view. It fails to recognize the importance of paradigm shifts in all spheres of Knowledge. It is a view which must be replaced by an understanding of the key competing paradigms affecting the organization and a charismatic vision of shifts in their importance. This vision must be charismatic in that emerging paradigms need advocacy and protection from their competition in order to be heard by Knowledge workers.

Transforming Leadership: Leadership in the transformal organization can only be charismatic. The very nature of the transforming process is such that imagination, vision, and advocacy are all requisites of effective leadership. This is not a religious charism, embodied only in one leader. It is shared charisma, which fuels the imagination of all members of the organization.

Transforming Imagination: Imagination, too, can be mundane. It can be characterized by ritualistic exercises which create future scenarios and test them against mechanistic organizations. The use of Imagination in this form will not produce the transformal organization. Instead, there must be a flow of ideas and visions directed by the spiritual energy of the organization and its members. Only in this way, can business leaders realize the dream of transformation where the global Quality of Life is enhanced through the conduct of business.

References

Agor, W. (1984) *Intuitive Management.* Englewood Cliffs, NJ: Prentice Hall.

Ammentorp, W. (1986) "Networks and Organization Design," *Proceedings*, INTERFACE 86, Atlanta, GA.

Anthony, E., et.al. (1988) *Envisionary Management.* New York: Quorum Books.

Ash, M. (1987) *Mary Kay.* New York: Harper and Row.

Buzzell, R. and Gale, B. (1987) *The PIMS Principles.* New York: Free Press.

Cohen, M., March, J. and Olsen, J. (1972) "A Garbage Can Model of Organizational Choice," *Administrative Science Quarterly.*

deChardin, P.T. (1977) *The Future of Man.* Fontana.

DeThomasis, L. (1987) *Faith, Finance and Society.* Memphis, TN: Christian Brothers College.

DeThomasis, L. (1989) *Monasteries on Wall Street: The Ten Commandments of Doing Ethics in Business.* Winona, MN: St. Mary's College.

DeThomasis, L. (1990) *The Collected Sayings of Brother Louis,* Winona, MN: Diocese of Winona.

Garrison, W. (1985) *NETWORK User's Manual.* Los Angeles, CA: CACI.

Hammermesh, R. (1986) *Making Strategy Work.* New York: J. Wiley.

Heilbroner, R. (1991) "Just Because Socialism Has Lost Does Not Mean That Capitalism Has Won," *Forbes,* May 27: 130–137.

Homer, J. (1985) "Worker Burnout: A Dynamic Model With Implications for Prevention and Control," *System Dynamics Review.* 1(1), pp. 42–62.

Huber, G. (1989) "A Theory of the Effects of Advanced Information Technology on Organizational Design, Intelligence and Decision Making," *Academy of Management Review,* 15(1), 47–71.

Kidder, T. (1981) *The Soul of a New Machine.* Boston: Little Brown.

Lyneis, J. (1982) *Corporate Planning and Policy Design.* Cambridge, MA.: MIT Press.

Mintzberg, H. (1989) *Mintzberg on Management.* New York: Free Press.

Morgan, G. (1986) *Images of Organization.* Newbury Park, CA: Sage.

Naffah, N. & Ellis, C. *Design of Office Information Systems.* North Holland.

Pope John Paul II (1991) "Centesimus Annus," *Origins* 21(1): 1–24.

Naisbitt, J. & Aburdene, P. (1986) *Reinventing the Corporation.* New York: Warner Publications.

Owen, H. (1987) *Spirit, Transformation and Development in Organizations.* New York: Abbott.

Schon, D. (1983) *The Reflective Practitioner.* New York: Basic Books.

Simon, H. (1977) *The New Science of Management Decision.* Englewood Cliffs, NJ: Prentice Hall.

Truitt, N. (1991) "Latin Bishops Look for Liberation in a Market Economy," *Wall Street Journal*, May 10: All.

United Nations (1991) Report on Human Development. New York: United Nations.

AFTERWORD

As a guide to readers, we have appended the table on the facing page which summarizes the paradigm shifts discussed in the preceeding chapters. We hope that it will stimulate business leaders to think about changes needed in their organizations and in the thoughts and actions of those who manage them. We recognize that the process of paradigm change is unfinished and that ours is but a first step toward new economic and social arrangements that are more closely in tune with the needs of the planet and its people.

This is an agenda which has been set free by the failures of socialism and the overthrow of repression. It is an agenda which democratic capitalism is uniquely fit to pursue. Turning again to "Centesimus Annus" we have, "If by 'capitalism' is meant an economic system which recognizes the fundamental and positive role of business, the market, private property and the resulting responsibility for the means of production, as well as human creativity in the economic sector, then the answer is certainly in the affirmative" (1991, p. 12). But, we must caution, it is precisely the freedom underlying democratic capitalism which must be carefully protected and transformed so that it flourishes and extends to all people. Else, capitalism's victory will be a short-lived transition to anarchy.

ALTERNATIVE BUSINESS
PARADIGMS FOR THE 1990s

ORGANIZATION DIMENSION	ALTERNATIVE PARADIGMS		
	COMMUNIST	CAPITALIST	TRANSFORMAL
PURPOSE	Satisfaction of Needs	Standard of Living	Quality of Life
OWNERSHIP & CONTROL	State	Shareholders	Stakeholders
MODE OF ORGANIZATION	Bureaucracy	Corporation	Cybernetic
PERFORMANCE	Quotas	Profits	Value
DIRECTION	Administration	Management	Leadership
PRIMARY RESOURCES	Labor	Technology & Capital	Knowledge
DYNAMIC	Ideology	Entrepreneurship	Imagination